Mary Atkins is the author of *Finding Your Voice: Ten Steps to Successful Public Speaking* and *Losing You*, a novel about overcoming adversity and the redemptive power of love. A Home Economist she is the Past President of the Australian Association of Food Professionals. Mary is also an award-winning speaker who currently travels the world lecturing on cruise ships.

A JOURNEY OF CREATIVE HEALING

A JOURNEY OF Creative HEALING

My story of resilience, remission and recovery through daily creative projects

MARY ATKINS

With a foreword by *Kimba Arem*

First published 2018

Copyright © Mary Atkins 2018

All attempts have been made to locate the owners of copyright material. If you have any information in that regard please contact the author at the address below.

All rights reserved. No part of this book may be reproduced by any mechanical, photographic, or electronic process, or in the form of a phonographic recording, nor may it be stored in a retrieval system, transmitted, or otherwise be copied for public or private use–other than for 'fair use' as brief quotations embodied in articles and reviews–without prior written permission of the publisher.

The author of this book does not dispense medical advice or prescribe the use of any technique as a form of treatment for physical, emotional or medical problems without the advice of a physician, either directly or indirectly. The intent of the author is only to offer information of a general nature to help you in your quest for emotional and spiritual well-being. In the event you use any of the information in this book for yourself, the author and the publisher assume no responsibility for your actions.

Mary Atkins
25 Curlew Way
Peregian Springs QLD 4573
Australia
Phone: 0414690880
Email: findingyourvoice@bigpond.com
Website: maryatkinsauthor.com

ISBN: 978 0 6481922 0 6

Internal design: Big Shed Creative Communications
Set in 11pt/16pt Minion Pro
Cover design: Big Shed Creative Communications
Cover image: Shutterstock

For my family, past and present

Contents

	Foreword	11
	Introduction	17
Chapter 1	Ordinary People Extraordinary Healing	21
Chapter 2	Road Map to MS and My Recovery	29
Chapter 3	Accepting Responsibility	41
Chapter 4	Understanding That My Life Had to Change Dramatically	61
Chapter 5	Rejecting the Diagnosis	71
Chapter 6	Stillness and Surrender	87
Chapter 7	Trusting and Acting Upon My Intuition	99
Chapter 8	Focusing on My Daily Creative Projects	109
Chapter 9	The Elephant in the Room: Radically Changing Your Diet	121
Chapter 10	The Six Steps to Healing	129
Chapter 11	Living and Learning	145
	Acknowledgements	155
	Bibliography	157

Foreword

**Kimba Arem, Music therapist, Molecular Biologist
and Recording Engineer**

'The wound is the place where Light enters you...'
Jalaluddin Rumi

It is not every day that you will encounter the material and perspectives on health and healing that you are about to read.

But it is my great hope that on the horizon people such as Mary and her extraordinary story will become commonplace.

It takes great courage to step off the trodden path, when all of life seems to fall away and there seems to be nowhere to turn. When we feel lost, all too often we seek the comfort of following in another's footsteps, especially those whose profession is authoritative and supposed to light our way. We follow the guidance of our societies' 'experts,' hoping they know where they, and therefore we, are headed ... but these fellow humans can often be just as lost in the jungle of life, bombarded with information overload and often lacking the living experience to validify the efficacy of choices deemed 'scientifically sound.'

As a practitioner of subtle energy and healing arts for 27 years—ignited by a near death experience in 1992—I too had to find my way through the labyrinth of seemingly unsolvable health challenges, with little truly helpful guidance. So now I find it natural to recognize words of experienced truth—breadcrumbs along the path of finding wholeness within—a major task for many of this in these changing times. Faced with increasing exposure to toxicities in the air we breathe and the foods we eat, chemicals in the water we drink, nuclear and electromagnetic radiation, and most of all, constant stress from the news, work, relationships…staying healthy has become challenging for many of us. Even with a biological lifespan of 120 years, it is a rarity for any of us to live to be 90 or 100. And I am told that mine is the first generation statistically unlikely to outlive our parents. Clearly humanity is in need of some behavioral modification. But underlying this behavior change is perhaps the need for a spiritual revival of sorts…a metaphysical crisis that could impel us towards potentially new octaves of evolution. It is interesting to note that the ancient Chinese word for 'crisis' is a composition of the two characters 'danger' and 'opportunity.'

Mary is among the new breed of humans who, when faced with overwhelming loss and life-threatening illness, took the leap of faith and decided to look within rather than without for answers—during a time before the internet. Despite what the outer world of reason and authority was urging her to do, she instead tapped into the under-used and extremely advanced system we each have built inside of the temple of our bodies—the 'inner-net.' Within us lies a mostly dormant faculty of knowing ourselves intimately—the intricately unique biology that is our body and it's needs, and the belief systems and thoughts that run though our often automatic-pilot wiring. We are told in the 'new age' that there is a mind-body connection that we have to cultivate—but in actuality the mind (which can loosely be defined as thoughts and emotions) is not separate from the body. Similarly, white light can be separated into the rainbow spectrum, but the colors we see only appear separate to our 3D consciousness—they are actually all the one white light. Therefore, it is inevitable that not only do our thoughts and emotions affect our physiology—they are truly not apart from it.

It is natural to understand that if we activate our whole mind-body system rather than isolated parts of it at one time (which is how the majority of humans currently operate), we form a coherence with all of the various aspects of ourselves, and from that perspective we can 'see' the whole picture and therefore know what needs changing, attention, or revision in our lives. As Mary outlines in her book—revealing the journey of self-discovery and the science that backs up her experience—there is nothing like creativity to ignite this level of expanded awareness. The act of creation—engaging the mind in novelty, listening to or creating music or other unique experiences—lights up not only the entire brain, but enlivens the Spirit and brings depth to the soul. Mary found this by taking the road less travelled—using creativity, silence, and other keys that her inner wisdom discovered—to cultivate optimum health and happiness.

We are blessed to learn from her heroine's journey back to wholeness.

We are undergoing a revolution on planet earth, nothing less than a complete rewiring of everything that has seemed to hold our world together—from the economy to societal structure, health care, education, ecological perspectives—right to the core of the very belief systems that have held sway for generations.

It is a time of radical transformation, and potentially the crisis is instigating the time of the great push—birthing humanity to a new level of symbiosis within the ecosystem of our bodies, and without—the ecosystem of our societies and planet Earth.

Perhaps you've heard the quote 'pain is inevitable, suffering is optional.' In this ever-changing river we call life on planet Earth, mental, emotional, and physical pains accompany us at various stages of the path. But to view these challenges as inherent, natural, and even purposeful for soul growth is the realization of the alchemical dream of turning lead into gold...

And as we see the rewards from looking within and creating the stillness to hear the quiet inner voice of wisdom, our confidence grows. In a world of immediate gratification and instant results, we can become discouraged if things don't seem to change or improve at the rate we have grown to expect. But a little quiet time observing nature and its cycles will show us that patience, perseverance, and a mustard grain of Faith pays off—in often unimaginably rewarding ways. The symbol of the lotus is a wonderful example of this—a pure, untarnished flower symbolizing beauty, truth, purity...and the soul's growth out of the murky compost of the challenges in life toward the sun of radiant self-realization.

In a time so in need of true elders to guide the coming generations, Mary is a shining example of someone who walks her talk, whose purpose in life is to serve and encourage others to be true to themselves.

Prepare yourself to embark on a journey into the life of a fellow seeker, such as yourself, who might have left some breadcrumbs for you along your path toward wholeness. And as you light your candle of inner truth, may you also be as a beacon to illuminate and inspire others. And together, may we collectively midwife each other into the birth of a new humanity, and create a new world of beauty and peace for our children, our children's children, and all of life.

Blessed be.

Kimba Arem
Music as Medicine
August 2017

www.gaearth.com
www.radiancehealth.com
www.secretofwaterthemovie.com

Introduction

In examining disease, we gain wisdom about anatomy and physiology and biology. In examining the person with disease, we gain wisdom about life.

Oliver Sacks, Neurologist, Naturalist, Historian and Author

I think anyone dealing with a serious illness has the same questions I did. Why me? And how did it happen to me? And is there a way back to good health?

Fifty plus years ago I was diagnosed with multiple sclerosis and after six years of suffering the debilitating disease I made a remarkable return to long-lasting health.

In a quest to find answers to questions that have long plagued me, I have laid bare my illness and recovery comparing my beliefs—why I became sick and how I recovered—with other key players. These are scientists who are opening our minds to the cause and effect of disease, holistic doctors who are on a similar crusade to identify characteristics of radical healing, medical reporters whose life work is to bring us the latest news on healing from around the world, and patients who have also made remarkable recoveries.

I was a World War II little'un, growing up in the London Blitz. My favourite bolt hole was under the kitchen table. There, being mindful of avoiding grown-ups' legs, I secretly listened to the adults' conversation as they voiced their fear of Hitler and all of his evil doings. I found it hard to understand if he was the source of all mankind's misery, why didn't somebody stop him? To me, it was as clear as the nose on my face once he was gone the war would be over. 'Why doesn't someone walk up to him and cut his head off with a big sword?' I would say to my imaginary friend when adults whispered the atrocities and misery of war. Living in a war-torn-scape was all I knew, and my view of it was tinged with a child's pragmatic innocence. So, the question mark was huge in my mind, the solution so simple, and yet adults seemed unable to either grasp or execute the concept.

As adults, our thoughts become a fortress of intellect, social and cultural values, skewed with our own limiting belief stories. We are like a teabag steeped for so long we become darker, more intense, and often more bitter. But childrens' simplistic views of life show wisdom way beyond their young years. 'Out of the mouth of babes,' we say.

As I age I have come full circle to value that inner child of mine—a naive voice of simplistic reason and it is with a resolve of innocent perspective I bring to this scrutiny, digging about in the entrails of an illness I suffered fifty years ago.

I have no perimeters or association to impede and impose on this investigation, except I have lived with, and subsequently had what is known as a radical healing from multiple sclerosis.

I write true to who am; out-of-the-mouth-of-a-babe lab rat, investigator, and recorder.

The book is not prescriptive or a how-to-manual, it is simply an anatomy of the attributes of my journey's six steps from ill health to full health, and a comparison of the relevant scientific findings in today's world. As such, there is a way for each of us to go home to our healing soul. There is no right way or wrong way, simply your way.

What I have found is the most amazing breadcrumb trail of scientific certainties and possibilities.

Chapter 1

Ordinary People Extraordinary Healing

'Don't be satisfied with stories, how things have gone with others. Unfold your own myth.'
Rumi, 13th-century Sufi Mystic

I hadn't visited the library since I became sick. Bluebells speckled the grounds of the library gardens on a spring morning in 1966. Nancy Sinatra's pop hit *These boots are made for walking*, blasted from a nearby open window. I lifted my pace.

Inside the ivy-clad building, books were stacked wide and high on their pine shelves, and the air traced a scent reminiscent of vanilla and beeswax.

At the desk, I asked for the opera section, specifically *La Boheme*. The librarian saw my arm slung tight across my chest in a sling and the young babies in the double stroller.

He instantly became my knight in shining armour, well at least a worn shiny suit, and went in search of the boxed records of the Puccini's opera, complete with the libretto.

At night as the children slept, I took myself to the opera, following the English translation of the libretto's story of a group of struggling artists living in the Latin Quarter of Paris in the mid-1800s.

My armchair became my magic carpet as the music and voices soared and I imagined looking down on the glassed roof garret in Paris and saw the palette of the attic-set somber and dark.

I had always wondered why people liked operas, but now I had given myself the gift of music, I began to understand. The music and exquisite voices revealed to me a new level of consciousness of the redemptive power of music. I was awash in a glory of emotion as the opera unfolded.

I was a girl more at home with the Beatles and pop music, but now I was in love with an opera and most definitely Puccini.

Twenty-four hours before my evening date with *La Boheme*, I had received a forceful intuitive message, a clear voice in my head said, 'plan, create, or do something every day you have never done before.'

My commitment from that point was to focus each and every day on a creative activity. It did not matter what, it was simply an exercise of doing something I had never done before. Each step to completion included conceptualizing, planning, action, and review.

I titled them 'daily creative projects,' which soon shortened to the more comfortable acronym DCP.

I believe this focus on a daily creative project was one of the key factors in my remarkable recovery from a debilitating illness.

Six months earlier, I had been diagnosed with an aggressive form of multiple sclerosis. The diagnosis was an answer to five years of unexplained episodic symptoms of weakness, numbness and paralysis, muscular and nerve spasms, headaches, blurred vision, and slurred speech.

I was not only physically incapacitated, but adding to the trauma, my husband Robert had died in a plane crash four years earlier, leaving me with our two infant children to raise on my own.

'I have good days and bad days,' I would say brightly to appease family and friends in the early years after Robert's death. They thought I was coping amazingly well, but inside I was a poor shadow of amazing, engulfed with grief, struggling with the responsibility of single motherhood, and trying to deal with an illness I was desperate to ignore. But eventually, I could no longer ignore, or hide, my dramatic deterioration in health. My left arm hung uselessly by my side, and I was dragging my left leg around the house like some drunken Quasimodo.

But now let's fast forward to 1967, nearly twelve months later when my neurologist was amazed and delighted he could find no trace of my previous multiple sclerosis symptoms and scarring.

He declared I was in remission.

I declared I was healed.

Dramatic healings or recoveries such as this are often given the prefix of 'spontaneous' or 'radical.' I hesitate when I use 'spontaneous' in connection with my healing, as mine was not of a biblical proportion of 'pick up your bed and walk' instant miracle. My remarkable recovery took time. Radical healing sits more comfortably, and I use the word 'healing' in its broadest sense of a process of recovery to good health once more. But for the purposes of this book, the terminology of spontaneous and radical healing is interchangeable.

These healings are not so uncommon as you would think. In my research, I found many inspirational and intriguing stories of people who have returned to good health after suffering chronic or life-threatening illnesses.

A good example is John Pattison from Newcastle upon Tyne, in the north of England.

John's home is the pretty coastal town of South Shields, on the mouth of the River Tyne. In 1974 as Harold Wilson's Labour party came back into power after four years of sitting on the cross-benches, John Pattison then aged eighteen received the prognosis the cancer of his lymphatic system was terminal. Immediately he was treated with chemotherapy and radiotherapy, which appeared to be successful, well, until the tumors returned, and three years later he suffered his fourth relapse. This time the doctors only offered palliative care to ease his final days.

Instead, John took himself off to the States where he stayed with an aunt in North Carolina for a few months. With time out, in a completely different and relaxed lifestyle, he started to feel well again. Upon his return to the UK, his specialist and doctors were amazed that all his tests were coming back negative. They declared him clear of cancer—and in remission.

'Being diagnosed and surviving cancer does give you a new outlook on life, and you don't take things for granted. You live each moment,' John Pattison said.

Living each moment, he gave up working as a shipyard worker to study nursing. Today, forty years on, he works as a Macmillan Cancer nurse specialist. And yes, he is still cancer free.

The western medical world has no answer for these occurrences, and invariably they are not documented in professional journals, or they are frequently dismissed as the patient is in remission or a misdiagnosis.

I tried to share my convictions about my healing with others, especially MS sufferers. But in those early years as I told my story, I grew tired of seeing people's eyes glaze over 'Yeah, yeah, sure she believes doing a daily bit of crochet or whatever healed her, but the answer is not that simple, let's see how long her remission lasts...'

But I knew with an unyielding certainty my Daily Creative Projects were a major player in my recovery.

Looking back now, I am convinced the key steps to my recovery were:

1. **Accepting responsibility**
   I had a resolute conviction my illness was symptomatic of

things that had gone on, and was going on in my life. In other words, I was responsible for my sickness, and who I was. (Chapter 3)

2. **Understanding that my life had to change dramatically**
I became aware that my sickness was transformative. It taught me the healing power of finding the 'silver-lining' in a situation. (Chapter 4)

3. **Rejecting the diagnosis**
I had a total resistance to accepting a diagnostic label. I always knew, with an inner wisdom, I would recover from whatever was making me sick. (Chapter 5)

4. **Stillness and surrender**
When the cluster of symptoms and grief overwhelmed me - I surrendered and let the stillness and quiet do the repair work required. (Chapter 6)

5. **Trusting and acting upon my intuition**
In the quiet place that sickness lays bare; my intuition gave me powerful messages. The messages were so forceful they could not be ignored. (Chapter 7)

6. **Focusing on my daily creative projects**
Creativity was my vehicle of choice to complete my recovery. I believe there is magic—in the power of focus, and the constancy of practice. (Chapter 8)

Each of these steps was vital for me to resurface to good health. Without these first four steps, (1. Accepting Responsibility, 2. Understanding that my life had to change dramatically 3. Rejecting the diagnosis, 4. Stillness and Surrender) I don't think I would have heard my intuition so clearly—directing me to commit to doing something creative each day—and equally, have been ready to act upon it. For others, whose stories I have read, their intuition spearheaded the changes they needed to make—to activate their own path back to wellness. We are all different.

Although we are unique, we all feel the same grip of fear and confusion when a major illness presents. But whether we embrace the expertise and knowledge of the medical world or find an alternative route, there are elements of anyone's return-to-health journey that can help others faced with a health crisis.

When you boil it all down, it is about survival—for people like me, survival means change, recovery, and spiritual growth. For others suffering chronic illness, it is primarily about acceptance and management of the disease, and for some, it is coming to accept and be at peace with—that survival is not an option.

The disease doesn't pop up like a mugger on a street, it is a long time in the making, well, it was in my case ...

Chapter 2

Road Map to MS and My Recovery

We are not meant to stay wounded. We are supposed to move through our tragedies and challenges and to help each other move through the many painful episodes of our lives.

Caroline Myss—Medical Intuitive, Author, Speaker

The blaze of fireworks over London's Trafalgar Square heralded in 1960. As we stood in the crowd of revellers, there was a sense the new decade promised dramatic change from the greyness of post-war life—the end of fourteen years of rationing and 'making do and mend' war-poster philosophy. With a newfound optimism, we felt it was time to free ourselves of old-hat social values and boundaries. As the last chime of Westminster's Big Ben rang out midnight, the 'swinging sixties' was born.

That beginning marked our debut as an engaged couple. Four-years after we met, Robert, my handsome wild colonial boy from Australia, proposed one summer day. 'I think it's about time, don't you?' he said as we looked into a vintage jeweller's window in the London Strand. He was my larrikin knight who came to save me from myself. He was fearless, pragmatic and worldly—he was my Rhett Butler to my muted but no less complex Scarlet O'Hara, minus the 'Ashley, Ashley, Ashley,' distraction.

We married a year later, 1961, in a medieval church, the breeze on our summer day prophetically lifting and tossing my long veil around us like a shroud, as man and wife we walked through the avenue of glossy green yew trees. We led the conga-line of guests across the lane to our joyous reception held in a sixteenth-century pub. It is one of the oldest pubs in England, and where, according to legend, Charles Dickens had written *Barnaby Rudge*.

Later we travelled the world on our honeymoon. I sound assured and entitled, don't I? But the truth is the illusion of happy-ever-after was no panacea for my continual battle with a sense of worthlessness and fearfulness. Combined with Robert's detached-adventure seeking view of life, it created an aching space between us as we visited intoxicating places that are no more, well, now have a new name or new territory.

Ten months after our wedding, our first child, a daughter we named Joanne, was born, and twelve months later in May 1963 our son, Neil arrived. We both wanted children, and it seemed we were well on target for a large family.

There were signs of my ill health with both pregnancies,

but only with hindsight could one identify them as episodes of multiple sclerosis.

My world stopped two weeks after the birth of Neil. Robert was killed in a light-plane crash. My life, I felt, was over, while the rest of the world relished in its 'peace-man-hippiness,' which spawned Woodstock, civil right marches and the rise of the Beatles.

Like most, I knew exactly where I was when President Kennedy was shot, I was at home, hand-washing nappies and struggling emotionally and physically to manage two babies on my own. I howled to the moon and back for Jackie K and myself.

You have already met little me in the Introduction, and so you would have read I was a nervous small child, made even more so by being bombed out of two homes and only comfortable when taking refuge under tables with my imaginary friend, who I carried around in a battered old attaché case.

The safety of being under the table originated from early in the war when we acquired a Morrison Shelter, which, when the all-clear sounded, acted as a table in the dining room. This heavy steel cage kept us safe when our home was bombed during the Blitz.

Today we would say my little child was suffering from post-traumatic stress disorder but in wartime, suffering was a matter of degree and mine would not have even raised an eyebrow.

By now you are getting the picture my ongoing biography was bound to be dysfunctional. Because of wartime, I did not commence my education until I was eight years old.

Amazingly I passed the 11+ exams and went to Grammar School. From 1944 to1976 the 11+ exams were taken in last year of primary school and the results indicated whether children were suitable candidates for secondary modern, technical, or the prestigious grammar school. Grammar school education was the only one that gave a youngster the opportunity of going on to University. But having achieved in primary school with two excellent teachers (Mr. Tinsley and Mr. Carter, I salute you) I struggled intellectually and socially in grammar school and left at fifteen to learn shorthand and typing.

I was useless as a stenographer and several poor employers had the acute disappointment of finding this out until at last, I realised shorthand typing was not where I should be.

With my mother's encouragement, I applied with many hundreds of other young women to become an air-hostess. Being an air-hostess back then was the pinnacle of glamour and worthy of getting your picture in the newspaper.

Much to my amazement, I was given the job.

In the late 50's and early 60's air travel, in general, was a far more rarefied experience than it is today. Yesteryear, there was no slobbing onto the plane in thongs, tee shirts, and tracksuit pants—people dressed up for the flight, wearing their smartest apparel like they were going on a Queen Mary transatlantic crossing. Passengers had plenty of leg-room, and experienced extraordinary service in comparison with today's airline travel—it was known as the 'Golden Age' of flying.

Sadly, back then, only single women were allowed to work as hostesses, and the company enforced our resignation shortly before marriage.

For a young woman who was reserved and ridiculously insecure, I found I was well suited to this job. My rostered routes were mainly West and East Africa. We worked hard—there was no twelve-hour limit on our days. Frequently, our flights to the more distant destinations were over two or more days, where en-route, we landed at a convenient destination and passengers were put up in local hotels before taking off the following morning. It was our responsibility as 'air-hostesses' to make sure they were cared for in transit.

Now I understand what the interview board saw in me, I was the wholesome-girl-next-door—eager to serve, eager to please—a natural.

Serving passengers served me. I was beginning to feel more comfortable with myself.

All was well in the skies. On the ground was a different matter. I was hyperventilating turning a peculiar shade of blue whenever I was a passenger in a car. The episodes were believed to be psychosomatic asthma attacks resulting from a spectacular head-on crash in Robert's brand-new sports car. Fortunately, neither of us was seriously hurt—physically—but with each subsequent car journey, my breathing or lack of it was becoming more dramatic.

Robert found a trendy psychiatrist in Harley Street.

The treatment was six overnight sessions in a clinic having success with the latest psychiatric treatment. I was given a single large dose of LSD injected into my butt late afternoon on each Saturday. Within minutes, I was tripping under the supervision of a psychiatric nurse for best part of six hours. Unlike Cary Grant, my all-time favourite matinee idol who supposedly had a love affair with acid, my sessions were psychedelic horror movies. A picture on the wall, prior to the needle, was of a yacht sailing serenely on an open sea but après jab the boat distorted into a fang-bearing tiger that leaped from the frame and the cream coloured walls became a jungle alive with fearsome creatures.

I cannot remember psychiatrist's face, but recall he always wore a polka-dot foppish bowtie, said, 'LSD is the new miraculous portal to the subconscious,' as my hands slowly dwarfed and dimpled and I became a virtual baby once more sucking my knuckles.

One weekend I relived being born—fantasising a difficult birth attended by a Frankenstein doctor. Cary G thought LSD was the path to truth and enlightenment, but for me, it was like being locked in a room with a homicidal maniac, and for years I had flashbacks of these terrors. On my last session, my psychiatrist said if my asthmatic attacks did not improve I would need to have more weekend sessions. Miraculously they stopped there and then! (The use of LSD in psychiatric treatment became illegal in the mid-1960s.)

Moving on to 1965, two-years after I was widowed, I was slim, people would say attractive, with a bit of a rounded tum but always nicely turned out. I wore my blonde hair in a fiercely backcombed geometric bob and dressed in high street copies of Mary Quant's signature design A-line shifts. My window (or widow) dressing was important to me because the rest of the store was falling apart, and looking good was the only thing I knew how to keep together. Appearance was pivotal in my avoidance of dealing with my grief. For me, the only time the pain of grief was diverted was when I was in the arms of a man. I was attracted to men as a drowning person is to a life raft. Which meant in the years following Robert's death, I had a few disastrous affairs.

People say twins are the hardest to raise in those first few years, but trust me the twelve months difference of my pigeon pair, who were at different stages of growth and needs is much less of a motherhood picnic - especially on one's own. As Jo was taking her first steps, Neil was still having night-feeds. As Neil was taking his first steps Jo was going through the 'terrible twos.' The time when brain development is expanding so rapidly, little ones are overwhelmed, and the only release they know is a ground-kicking tantrum.

The responsibility of single parenting overwhelmed me.

Soon my life was spiralling out of control. I was exhausted with my destructive way of avoiding grief, single parenting, and the now more frequent episodes of numbness, muscle spasms, and clumsiness.

In September 1965, a couple of days before my twenty-seventh birthday the MS symptoms, like pendulum waves, all moved as one to take me down. My disease was in full bloom and could no longer be ignored. I was well and truly sick.

Multiple sclerosis is a heavyweight disease. It is a disease of the central nervous system with random painful and incapacitating symptoms that may stay for a while or linger longer. The medical world does not know what causes MS, and there is no known cure.

It is not an easy disease to diagnose and today the neurologist's arsenal of tools includes an MRI, spinal taps and electrical tests to help determine if MS has affected nerve pathways.

Fifty years ago, the only diagnostic tools for determining neurological ills were a pocket torch, a rubber mallet, a pin and a lumbar puncture. For a diagnosis of multiple sclerosis to be reached there had to be significant scarring and medical history to support the diagnosis, and that I had in spades.

Even today with MRI, scanning and blood tests, there is no single test that is proof positive for diagnosing the disease. In my case, the neurologist simply had the full-blown presenting symptoms. He considered the symptoms present at the time of my consultation particularly aggressive and gave me notice I would be wheelchair bound within a short period of time. The second opinion from another reputable neurologist gave me the same prognosis.

What was the song with the line 'Just call me a cock-eyed optimist?' No matter, it summed me up completely. I did not believe the diagnosis. When my GP wanted me to join an MS support group I obstinately refused. I told him I believed my illness was about my lifestyle, difficult pregnancies and births of my two beautiful children, and the shock and grief of losing my reckless wonderful champion.

Within weeks I was bedridden. Those were the dark days in that first winter after being diagnosed with multiple sclerosis when I could not lift my head off the pillow. My limbs were so heavy I could not roll onto my side. I could only lay flat on my back with my arms and legs splayed. Sleep was dense. If I dreamt I had no recall. When eventually a twitch of a muscle or nerve breached the stupor, I began to wake but my eyelids seemed as though they had been glued together, and once more I retreated into sleep.

Fortunately, my mother and sister stepped in to care for my children and myself, and gradually as the weeks passed the healing sleep and rest allowed my energy to creep back. During those months of hibernation, I had occasional days where I felt strong enough to get up and contribute in a small way. But always there was the dull ache of useless limbs with frequent tics of stabbing pain.

In the new-year, I was able to make breakfast for the children and spend the morning with them. At lunchtime when they had their midday sleep, I was so played out I once more became a one-armed Quasimodo, hunched and dragging my leg behind me, shuffling to bed to rest. Some days were better than others, but I was always hopeful even with the inconsistency of progress that I was on the mend.

One early spring morning as the crocuses were crowning in the garden to greet a watery sun, my sister had taken the children for a play date with their cousins.

It was a momentous morning, an event, which will forever stain my memory.

I was resting on the settee in the lounge listening to my favourite recording of Rimsky Korsakov Scheherazade. After Robert's death, I played this piece frequently—the music comforted and eased my spirits. The crescendos of brass, aching intensity of the woodwinds, and sweet violins filled my senses as I rested. With each passage of the music, I slipped easily into a dream-like state. My mind gently played, peeling back the sounds to imagine the conductor, like some great puppeteer, weaving his imprint on the music. Deeper and deeper I sank into the cushioned settee, my being filled with the familiar sweet refrain of the solo violin.

The message came with such clarity. The words were spoken in my head with such insistent authenticity I could not ignore them.

'You are right not to give credence to the diagnosis of your illness. Your body is simply creating symptoms reflecting your deepest fear of being alone and of not being capable to shoulder the burden of the responsibility of raising two children on your own.'

It was a moment when a biblical model of a loving God swept the wispy clouds apart from on high and spoke directly to me. The voice's timbre and the sound were redolent with a majesty and presence and not for a second could I doubt the authority of the message.

It was my shooting star zipping through a black star-lit night, my ride on the back of a jet-ski as I eye-balled a blue whale in the Pacific Ocean, and my road to Damascus moment all rolled into one.

I rested for a while, relishing the bliss flowing through me. Gradually I opened my eyes and found the dull orange fabric of the settee now had the vibrancy of a Buddhist monk's robes.

My limbs felt stronger as I sat up and swung my legs to the floor. It was if I was seeing the room for the first time—everything was so much clearer, sharper and vital. I walked over to the window. The day was overcast, and a finger of the sun was valiantly breaking through the overcast sky. Again, a voice filled my senses—this time the message was in the first person.

'I need to put my focus on being creative. Yes, a creative project. I need to create something new each day. It doesn't matter what—I simply need to focus on the planning and joy of creativity.'

I did not doubt my intuition for a second. I knew this was what I needed to do.

My thoughts never implied this was a healing path.

I was consumed only with a need to be creative, and to do it daily.

I defined my DCP (daily creative project) as something new and unique I had not experienced, made or performed before. Each day unfolded with a sense of purpose. I planned, researched, executed, and marveled at my work.

Projects were as simple, as you have previously read, as discovering the beauty and mystery of an opera. Challenging my map reading skills—to find some new locale to take the children on a specially designed picnic. Writing short stories. Making papier-mâché toys with the children. Creating a floral arrangement. Painting and decorating the children's nursery furniture. Renovating a set of dining room chairs. Trying some new cooking technique. Making patchwork cushion covers. Some took major planning to bring to fruition, some were easier than others—especially the DCP's in the early days—but always my focus was on the pleasure of creating and the fulfillment of completion.

With each passing week, I was growing stronger. My dragging left leg had healed and my left arm that had lurked so long in a sling was now free to hold a knitting needle or an embroidery needle. My vision was good, and I no longer sounded like a drunk at a party.

The healing was completed and confirmed with a visit a year later to both neurologists. Both found no trace of symptoms and declared I was in remission.

I declared I was healed and in good health. Not only in good bodily health but mind, body and spirit were now functioning at a new level of stability and contentment. I no longer needed a man to define me to ease the grief. The responsibility of raising my children singlehandedly sat comfortably upon me. I had found acceptance in my lot. In short, I was functioning and at ease with myself.

That was over fifty years ago, and my health has been pretty good since then. Today I am still working as a destination and enrichment lecturer on cruise ships—lucky me.

But don't think I am one of those incredible older women you see on social media who will still be pole dancing at ninety because I am not. Don't think that I see myself as some sort Grandma Moses guru that has bearded all my demons because I haven't, and I know I will still be working on being a grown up till I fall off the twig.

The only link today, that may be evidence of my past illness, is a condition called peripheral neuropathy that affects my feet which my doctor believes may have been caused by the MS so many years ago. (Peripheral neuropathy is a disorder that occurs when these nerves malfunction because they're damaged or destroyed.)

But for an old girl—who has packed a lot of living into my four score years—I am in relatively good shape!

Chapter 3

Accepting Responsibility

'In the long run, we shape our lives, and we shape ourselves. The process never ends until we die. And the choices we make are ultimately our own responsibility. '
Eleanor Roosevelt—First Lady, writer, activist, diplomat, humanitarian

A few years back, I remember listening, mouth gaping, to a radio shock-jock broadcaster who denied that stress was real. As caller after caller identified their stress events, you could almost hear the pages of the thesaurus rustling as he searched for stress synonyms. 'It's anxiety,' he explained to one listener. His pedantry knew no bounds, pressure, tension, nervousness, unhappiness, and even 'that is not stress, it's being in a rush,' he says to another caller. Having insulted all his callers and no doubt raised their stress thresholds, he concludes the feisty debate with 'I'll say it again there's no such thing as stress!'

But the Austrian born scientist is known as the 'Father' of stress research, Dr Hans Selye, MD, PhD, DSc, FRS who coined the medical use of 'stress' in 1936 may have, in some small way, agreed with him.

Selye, affectionately known as the 'Einstein of medical research' wrote 33 books and 1,600 articles on the effects of stress on health. He spoke eight languages fluently but was always conflicted that he had given the title of 'stress' to this particular medical condition. He said if English had been his first language, he would have called it 'strain.' As 'strain' would have described it better. He always contended that 'stress' was 'the spice of life,' and that 'it is not stress that kills us, it is our reaction to it.'

His finding on the effects of stress was serendipitous when as a young endocrinologist in Prague he was working on a laboratory experiment with rats with the purpose of isolating a new ovarian hormone. While he failed in isolating the new hormone, his experiments showed him something more. Where other scientists would quit at this stage and move onto the next definitive study, this creative and original thinker took a harder look and discovered a common powerful indicator that biological stress was a real threat to the rat's health—and by way of analogy, ours as well.

He died in 1982 at the age of 75 having had an illustrious career that included being director of the International Institute of Stress at the University of Montreal. Selye's average workday was 10 to 14 hours, including weekends and holidays. He habitually got up around 5:00 a.m. or earlier, took a dip in the small pool in the basement of his house, and then rode his bicycle six miles to work. Somehow this powerhouse of man managed to find time to court and marry three times, raise a family of five children, and go dancing. But first and foremost, he was married to his work.

'Stress in health and disease is medically, sociologically, and philosophically the most meaningful subject for humanity that I can think of.' (Hans Selye)

We all get stress in some way or other, from the smallest irritation of trying to get service over the phone to having an argument with a work colleague or worse family, moving to a new home, loss of a job, road accidents, financial woes, divorce, bereavement right through to the constant running mind-tape of our limiting beliefs.

The scientific and medical world has been aware for well over half a century that constant stress damages the body. In fact, the World Health Organisation reported in 2008 that stress will be the health epidemic of the twenty-first century.

So, what happens under stress? According to Selye, there are three stages in the process: alarm reaction, resistance, and exhaustion.

Take an example of public speaking, which is known as an extreme stress for many. The terror of being the centre of attention at a lectern for many people is undeniable.

In the first stage, the brain goes to mush, the mouth becomes dry, the heart races, the stomach churns, the pupils dilate, you feel nauseous, your body shakes, and you have an overriding urge to run to the toilet.

All of these symptoms or manifestations of fear are known as the 'fight-or-flight' syndrome where a hormonal cocktail of adrenaline and cortisol is pumped into the bloodstream to provide more energy reserves to call upon—readying you for action.

But the good news for speakers once you speak, the symptoms subside. This is the second stage where the body begins to repair the damage done by the arousal, and normally the stress symptoms vanish.

Our cavemen ancestor, protected only with his wooden spear, would have found this response to fear readied him for the hunt. Fear would have triggered the release of hormones causing his pulse to quicken. His lungs would take in more oxygen to fuel the muscles, his blood sugar would increase, his pupils would dilate, his digestion would slow and perspiration increase. But once the threat had passed these levels of hormones that pumped through his body would return to normal.

Unfortunately, this early part of our brain that triggers the 'fight and flight' response cannot tell the difference between a charging woolly mammoth and a two-hour call to a service worker, whose English is poor but the ability to stick to the company script is not. For some, it may be trying to solve a computer glitch, in others, a disagreement with a fellow worker.

In this third stage, when these stressors are a constant part of life, the 'fight-or-flight' response does not shut off—the body's adaptive energy eventually runs out, and exhaustion sets in. The exhaustion can lead to a breakdown in the functioning of vital organs, causing disease and if the stress continues—death.

Let's face it living in this world is stressful.

Occasionally we might fantasize about a stress-free life in the country, with an overflowing veggie patch growing organics, a doe-eyed cow in the pasture ready to give us raw milk, chickens free-ranging in the paddock, and a comfortable living simply a million miles away from care.

But life is not perfect; possums may eat the organic veggies, your chickens may stop laying, you could get salmonella from your raw milk or be anxious that your neighbour's genetically modified crops may affect your market sales of homegrown produce.

Your ancient part of the brain is having a field day—adrenaline and cortisol pumping as you are stressed to the limit.

But if you were to view each as one as life's challenges, rather than 'woe is me' would it make a difference to health? The answer is a resounding 'yes.'

Professor Wendy Berry Mendes PhD, a psychologist at the University of California in San Francisco, has found that if we reframe the way we look at stress—seeing it as a 'challenge' rather than a 'threat' the benefits are that it allows us to recover from a 'fight-or-flight' episode more effectively.

Her studies show that the 'threat' response which she links to a sense of fear—is the response that does the damage. But her studies have also shown that mild to moderate bursts of 'challenge' stress with a recovery period, is similar to the benefits of physical exercise, and can make us stronger and more resilient. (*Cure: A Journey into the Science of Mind Over Body*—Jo Marchant, published in 2016)

One of these studies focused on the fear of public speaking. Some people taking part were given information about the advantages of the body's stress response and were encouraged to re-interpret their bodily signals during the public speaking task to see them as beneficial. They were also asked to read summaries of three psychology studies that showed the benefits of stress. The others in the study received no information about reframing stress to a challenge. It was a pretty demanding test—they were given three minutes to prepare a five-minute speech, which they had to present to 'bad-cop' judges who shook their heads disapprovingly, while continually scowling. The unsupported group found the test fearful, stressful—a threat. The group that was given the benefits of stress and reframed the stressful exercise to a challenge, weathered the trial well, reporting that they felt they had more resources to cope with the indomitable task of presenting a public speaking task to a hostile audience.

The 'Father of Stress', Hans Selye, many decades earlier said the same thing: 'stress is not necessarily something bad, it all depends on how you take it.'

Rick Hanson PhD is a neuropsychologist, a Senior Fellow of the Greater Good Science Center at UC Berkeley, and a *New York Times* best-selling author. In his book *Hardwiring Happiness: The New Brain Science of Contentment, Calm and Confidence*, published in 2013, he writes that our brains have a negative bias. This negative bias is a survival technique within the earliest part of our brains, developed to avoid danger.

He explains that our distant ancestors lived with daily, minute-by-minute threats of being wounded or killed by a predator or other natural hazards and it seemed this threat concentrated their brains crucially on danger and survival.

The good stuff like 'their eyes met across a crowded cave,' a feast of a woolly mammoth, or even the shelter and warmth of a fire, were not as high priority as survival.

So first and foremost, being focused on the danger to keep safe was passed on down through the generations.

Hanson's work showed clearly that our brains are pigs-in-the-mud if our limiting belief mind-tapes are triggered by events or situations. As Hanson said, 'the brain is like Velcro for negative experiences, but Teflon for positive ones!'

This means that even today with our sophisticated neocortex part of the brain, which is responsible for abstract thought, language and imagination, if someone compliments us: 'Love the new outfit, really slims you down' instead of pleasure, we are inclined to ruminate on the last few words. 'Really slims you down' equals, 'she thinks I am fat.'

So now it is time to put 'me' under the microscope, to investigate why I got sick.

My first birthday, in 1939, was celebrated on the day Neville Chamberlain declared that Britain was at war with Germany. Shortly after this, my father joined the army and was posted to London as an officer in the Royal Artillery.

We lived in a suburb close to London, and during the Blitz, our home was destroyed in the bombing. My mother, sister and I sheltering under the solid iron Morrison shelter in the dining room, were lucky to escape with a few minor injuries from flying glass.

With no home and no belongings, my maternal grandfather,

who lived a few miles away, gave us refuge. He was a crusty, self-made man who suffered the loss of his young son and beloved wife a year apart. My mother was just thirteen.

My four-year-older sister was his favourite. I think her dark hair; soulful brown eyes and spirited personality reminded him strongly of my grandmother. He found it hard to extend the love to his second grandchild, a timid withdrawn child as I was then, who peeped at life from behind her mother's skirts. He was tough on me, telling me frequently and in so many ways that I was inadequate.

Being so little, I lived my life through the eyes of my mother, whom I adored. She was a gentle, kind, generously loving mother, but was completely dependent on her father. She grew up in a middle-class home and endured the grievous losses of her older brother and mother at a young age. As a young woman, she was not allowed to work, and her socialising was restricted. In short, her father dominated her. So, the game was set, she tried to protect me as best as she could from seeing his disapproval—'he is only joking darling'— but was never able to confront him, and I swallowed whole his view of me. His style of grandparenting was harsh, and while he never lifted a hand to me his words were continually abrasive. 'One day I will cut off your wallapolupa (head),' was his frequent tease.

I retreated into a fantasy world where I shared myself only with my imaginary friend 'Sonny,' who I carried around in a small brown attaché case.

For a while, during the war, we became camp followers. My father commanded the artillery regiment that defended Chequers, the country retreat of Winston Churchill, and he also spent time in Wales as an artillery instructor. We took rooms in an assortment of billets close to where he was. A room in someone's home became our home, where we lived out of suitcases and had meals when it suited the house owners to allow us to use the kitchen. We saw my father for the odd hour or so from time to time, but I never truly knew him until I after the war ended and he was demobbed.

Hitler launched his last offensive on London, in the summer of 1944. This bombardment came in the shape of long-range missiles titled V-1 and V-11 flying bombs. These were grimly nicknamed 'doodlebugs.' Their buzzing drone of a motor announced their presence overhead and when the jet engine fuel ran out, the bomb simply fell from the sky—seconds of sheer, terrifying silence before the bomb exploded on impact. We were running for the Anderson shelter in neighbour's garden when the bomb hit, and Grandfather's house was partially destroyed in the explosion. We once again escaped with a few grazes and cuts, which came from being lifted by the blast and thrown across the length of the lawn.

Looking at this time in my life more critically, the best part of those early years the dominant male in my life was a man who found it hard to relate to me. The female was unable to protect me from me from his disapproval.

The other male in my life, my father—to a small child—seemingly abandoned me when he went to war. He came into my life again properly at the age of eight. He was a man of strong conservative values, but a kindly man who tried to set my world aright, but the dye was already set—I was an emotionally impoverished child, clutching for approval.

Add to these stresses—fear, homelessness, deprivation, and trauma of wartime—and this was the crucible, I believe, where my identity was formed.

My fear of disapproval was locked into my psyche so powerfully that I believed I needed to please others to survive. And if I met with disapproval at any time, I would blame and self-hate before retreating into my inner world. Denial is a safe haven when you are in pain.

In my teenage years, I was attracting situations into my life where those limiting beliefs could be reinforced. At Grammar School I floundered, and later when I joined the work-force, I moved unsuccessfully from job to job. I continually blamed myself for my inadequacies. As my hormones kicked-in, I formed relationships with the opposite sex—none were functional.

My parents' generation was hopeless in giving their children a sex talk. It never happened. I had little knowledge of sex except what I had learned behind the primary school shed. For this, our little group of nine-year-olds was shamed and given five strokes of the cane across our hands by the Headmaster for our 'smutty' talk.

It was up to my older sister to explain what was happening to me when I arrived home from an outing as a young teenager, distressed with my skirt covered in blood. Periods were something we did not talk about at home.

The Dr White sanitary napkins, white inflexible planks of things, were placed on the top-most shelf in the airing cupboard to make sure my father was not embarrassed or offended by the sight of them.

Bizarre times and their generation's attitude to women only skewed my emotional development to believe our sexual function and desires equalled shame. When Robert came into my life in my late teens, he was everything I wasn't. He knew his mind, was disciplined, confident and socially adept—as the lyrics of Kenny Rogers song said, 'He knew when to hold them and when to fold them.' And to me, the fearful mouse of a young girl, he was a courageous giant of a man, made even more exciting as he loved flirting with physical danger.

In the movie theatres at this time was the film *Sundowners*, with Robert Mitcham playing the role of a wanderlust drover taking his family from town-to-town in outback Australia— this added another unrealistic layer of appeal to my Antipodean hero. I saw Robert as the most wonderful symbol of freedom.

He reset my boundaries, 'if you are late again Mary I won't wait,' and he kept his word no matter what the consequences. There were echoes of my grandfather's firm handedness, which to my surprise made me feel secure. Why then was this hero of a man interested in the Mary of this particular seven-year incarnation? A young woman who was so fearful of life I found it hard to eat or drink in social situations because my hands shook so much, and I was so painfully withdrawn I hardly said a word. A friend of Robert's once said to me I was the most abstemious person they had ever met. I had no idea why Robert was mine. He was simply the most exquisite enigma to me.

No doubt about it we humans are fashioned by many layers of stories, our psyche worn and ragged like a coastline shaped by the weather and ocean. We are an emotional jigsaw, constantly looking for a matching piece, to build or deconstruct our picture. In short, in our egoic state, we are complex.

And without a doubt, my champion had his own emotional baggage. He found it hard to say, 'I love you,' in fact, he never once said it in all our five years together. Even today, I find it painfully sad he went to his death without being able to commit his heart. But I will always remember the way his eyes looked lovingly at me as I came down the aisle on my father's arm.

Robert came from a family where order and control were key to its function. Both parents were professionals, and their children were raised in a household where discipline and being 'right,' and 'doing the right thing' was paramount. He was expected to follow in his father's footsteps to become a surgeon, instead, after a year of enforced medicine at the university, he transferred into dentistry.

I believe Robert was intrigued by the love I was able to show but primarily was attracted to my dependence upon him. He grew up knowing only control, and this was the emotional jigsaw piece, which locked us together.

I loved him beyond measure. 'He was my north, my south, my east and west, my working week and my Sunday rest, my noon, my midnight, my talk, my song.' W. H. Auden's poem expresses how I felt about him. Simply he was my life.

I was compliant with all of his decisions, which he made for us both, after all, he was so assured, he was brighter, cleverer, and stronger than me. He was his own man—when he wanted to play sports, have a poker night out with boys, fly his plane— he did it. He had a strong sexual libido and did not understand when I had a 'headache.' The headaches came before we married after an abortion, which Robert believed was the right thing to do. The night before he died we argued about sex, well…I did the hysterical wrangling, while he maintained a controlled and dismissive stance. My rejection of him the day before he died and his distant response, as well as the unresolved shame and anger of the abortion, without doubt, muddied the pool of my grief.

Abortion is such a controversial issue. We see it as either a mortal sin or conversely a woman's right to make this call at a time when she feels there is no other option but termination, and no guilt should be attached.

I will try to be as honest as I am able regarding this moment in my life. I say, 'honest as I am able' as in the 1960's the groundswell of disgust—and I mean disgust in all its guises of repugnance, loathing, and revulsion—came from the church, the righteous anti-abortion lobbyists, and the masculine in society—made it hard for a woman to qualify her real feelings about an illegal termination of a pregnancy.

It was a time when reproduction was an area controlled by the medical world, a time when the medical world was mainly men. Single women were denied the birth control pill—the only option being condoms or a diaphragm. Abortion was a criminal act, and as such carried sentences of five to ten years for the abortionist, and a possible three years for the mother.

Today, I see the guilt I felt back then was more about how society and myself viewed sexuality and pregnancy outside of marriage. Being pregnant outside of marriage was deeply shameful, a corrupt politician had more credibility than a girl in the early sixties who lost her cherry before she promised to obey at the altar. Then, add to this the criminal act of a back-street abortion, and you are well and truly dammed.

So now fifty plus years on am I remorseful I had this termination? Yes—but you cannot undo what is done, and yesterday was a distant country.

The coroner recorded that Robert's death was due to pilot inexperience.

The weather was fine the day of the accident. Indeed, it was a bright and sunny afternoon when Robert climbed into the Cessna and completed his checklist. His purpose was to get his hours up to retain his pilot license. His log showed he planned to do 'circuits and bumps' which means the pilot goes through the procedures of take-off, doing a circuit of the airfield before landing the plane, and without stopping guns the plane once more down the runaway, to keep repeating the sequence.

But shortly after Robert took off, the cloud cover came down, and with no visual landmarks to guide him—it was assumed—he became lost. A witness reported the plane was seen low in the sky below the clouds—obviously, the reduced altitude was to get his bearings—before the small plane was heard climbing too steeply. It stalled at the top of the climb and nose-dived into an unoccupied block of units in southwest London.

Gradually after the initial gut-wrenching heartbreak of his loss, my grief turned to anger. I remembered the car crash we had where we were lucky to get out of it alive. I remembered the time he raced dangerously with another high-powered car on the motorway using the handbrake to slow us, so they did not see our car's brake lights as they tailgated us at high speeds.

I remembered pettily other risks he took, suddenly he was no longer the wild colonial boy who had excited me with his daring, now I could only brokenheartedly see irresponsibility.

I hated that he had left me to raise our two small children on my own—when your default system is set to incapable and not enough, that is a heavy burden to carry. But most of all, I was angry; as I felt he had abandoned us.

I dreamt of him often, but frequently it was seeing him walking in the distance, never looking back. One night I dreamt I caught up with him and asked him why he had left me. He did not answer, just shook his head and walked on. For years, I found it hard to speak of him or the accident, because my body shook uncontrollably, and my breathing became so shallow I was gasping for breath. So, I avoided questions about him, about grief, and how I was faring. Complicating this was my need to please, so I would never voice my anger to people outside of my family, in case they disapproved.

By now, you are getting the picture of a mess of a young woman. I had no bedrock of self-esteem and layered confidence in myself to draw on. And I slipped more into the morass of being needy. I became desperate for solace with other men, finding the only time I could avoid the pain was when I was in bed with them.

My stress levels were hurricane force six, and constant.

My illness showed me clearly what my identity had been saying in my head for years—now I truly was incapable, I was not enough, and I was powerless.

Dr Bruce Lipton PhD is a cellular biologist of considerable reputation. His research and ongoing quest for understanding the cell's processing systems led him to examine the principle of quantum physics. He is the author of four books including *The Biology of Belief: Unleashing the Power of Consciousness, Matter and Miracles*, published in 2005, which is an exciting and reasonably lay-friendly read, leaving you in awe of the complexity and genius of our cells.

But the best part is, he gives us scientific evidence of the potential of how our minds and cells in our bodies can change what we perceive as our destiny.

His research provided evidence that our genes and DNA do not control our biology—instead, our DNA is controlled by signals from outside the cell, including oft-repeated messages emanating from positive and negative thoughts. He found that our consciousness conclusively affects the biochemistry of the body, moment by moment.

> 'Cells, tissues, and organs do not question information sent by the nervous system. Rather, they respond with equal fervor to accurate life-affirming perceptions and to self-destructive misperceptions. Consequently, the nature of our perceptions greatly influences the fate of our lives.' *Spontaneous Evolution: Our Positive Future and the Way to Get There From Here*—Bruce Lipton, PhD and Steve Bhaerman, published in 2010.

Another prominent neuroscientist, working in the field of brain chemistry was Candace B Pert PhD, who found that the mind and our emotions affect health. In her book, *Molecules of Emotion: The Science Behind Mind-Body Medicine*, published in 1997, she promoted a more holistic approach to understanding health. 'I've come to believe that virtually all illness, if not psychosomatic in foundation, has a definite psychosomatic component,' she wrote.

Accepting I was responsible for my physical and emotional health did not come easily.

Immediately following Robert's death, I was fortunate to have the support of an older relative, Aunty G. She had lost her husband in her mid-forties and was a wise counsellor. 'You have a choice, you can either decide to become bitter and miserable for the rest of your life, or you can accept your loss, rise above it and become stronger.' The thought of being as miserable and dysfunctional as I was then, spurred me on. I desperately wanted to accept my loss so I could 'rise above it.'

But for four years I was stuck in the grief process—coping poorly with guilt, anger, and denial.

I was angry with Robert for dying and abandoning me, I was angry with myself for not being more of a wife while he was with me, I was angry I had to carry the sole burden of two infant children. But most of all, I was ashamed of not being the perfect parent to my children.

I was a long way from reaching the holy grail of acceptance of the loss of my health and the loss of Robert.

I honestly did know how to get there emotionally. But my desire to change was stronger than the conflict.

I blamed myself for my sickness, conclusively I saw it was my fault. Today I understand that this was simply another dress-up of my ego's guilt stories that constantly plagued my mind since childhood. This chronic breast-beating and blame was the complete opposite of the healthier end of the spectrum—maturely taking responsibility for my part in the drama.

I had a powerful glimpse of my reality before sickness confined me to bed. One day, a mug of coffee in hand, I was mindlessly overseeing my children play, my mind consumed with the usual default screen of anxiety. As the children played, Neil tripped over one of his toys, I watched Jo carefully pull him to his feet and clasp him in a bear hug as she patted his back. Pat-pat, there-there, pat-pat, there-there. Like a lightning-strike—my eldest child was being the mum. BOOM! Where had I been? And how could I have ever lost sight being present for my babies?

They say that you see your life in a flash before you physically die, but that could equally be said of this moment in my life. I needed this intervention, this clarity of intuition, to open my eyes to the destructive nature of my thinking and lifestyle, and to recognise that I could not sink lower. My emotional resources were depleted—I had hit rock bottom. Change was inevitable.

It was then my illness took over.

As I became more and more dependent on others, at first all I could do was sleep. As my energy slowly returned, I spent time caring for my children. I can't remember ever reading a book or watching television. I was deeply quiet both in mind, body, and spirit. I was too tired to have any fight within me. My mind and body were in survival mode.

I single-mindedly held onto a faith or a vision that I would come through this.

There are no easy steps I can offer to reach this release of attachment to the pain or unhappiness. For me, it was a culmination of emotional rollercoasters, before the fight and conflict were no more and I was at one with my illness. There was a lot to mend, a central nervous system that was compromised, no resolution to my grief, and fears of being a single parent.

Throughout my young life, I had always leaned on others to direct and dictate my life choices, so you see, it was vital for me to change. The first step was coming to the point of acceptance of all I had been emotionally avoiding.

Acceptance did not mean waving the white flag, as I disappeared under the weight of it all. Accepting responsibility for my illness was interlaced with facing the chronic fear of raising two children on my own. Once I faced these fears of not being strong enough, well enough to be a single parent, they no longer had the power to hold me in their sorry grip.

Any personal change is hard won, and in my agonising trek to acceptance, I found that intellect is a poor second in a quest to reach the peace of acceptance. I might not understand it, or be able to qualify or quantify it, but the balm of acceptance—I alone, was responsible—came to me during this time of stilled hibernation.

The consensus of extensive studies of other radical survivors shows that a key step in their recovery was taking responsibility or control of their health management.

As the weeks grew into months, this act-of-grace of acceptance allowed me to see that my sickness was a gift, an intervention if you will, that regenerated a new and better version of me.

Chapter 4

Understanding That My Life Had to Change Dramatically: Finding the Silver Lining

'The wound is where the light enters you'
Rumi—13th Century Sufi Mystic

At the age of sixteen, I found God. Or, I should say, I experienced the power of the evangelical call when Billy Graham came to preach the gospel at London's Wembley Stadium, known fittingly as the cathedral of English soccer.

My word—Billy was a powerful orator. Like so many in the audience, tears coursed down my cheeks and my heart cried out for redemption. The reverend's voice, resonant with authority charged us 'to invite Jeeee-suss into your heart, God is calling you now my brothers and sisters, our pastoral assistants are waiting to help you reach out to your Savior.'

So many folks, heads bowed, hands clasped reverently, made their way down into the arena for salvation. But I was in turmoil—the wounded me was crying out to follow, but the other me—so bound up in wanting to conform with people who drank hot chocolate before bedtime (my parents and their conservative peers) and who also believed faith was a crutch—held me back.

The flow of supplicants did not cease, and I could no longer ignore my need to assuage the rawness Billy had opened. I went down into the arena. We lined up silently, waiting for our assistant to talk us through our commitment to God, but once with the impassioned young worker, the glow of redemption gradually lost its shine as he took my details and advised I should be on guard in these early stages. I should read my bible regularly, and know the doubts when they came would be the Devil's work, and I should redouble my prayers and bible readings.

By the third day, my apologies to the believers—I had failed in my fervour. But this brief dalliance with a power supposedly greater than the sum of us gave me the portal to explore my own brand of spirituality for the rest of my life.

So, when the 'spiritual wake-up' call came with my decline in health, it was not a foreign experience. I had been there before.

The advice my Aunty G gave me in those early days of grieving was powerful stuff. I might not have recognized it then, but I see clearly that her pragmatic guidance provided

A JOURNEY OF CREATIVE HEALING

me with the determination to grow stronger. For good measure, she threw in another homespun goodie. 'Every dark cloud has a silver lining. The trick is, darling, to find the silver lining.'

Some people do recognise sickness is the line in the sand that helps make beneficial changes in their lives. Writing this chapter takes me right back to the conflict I experienced when Billy called me. I badly want to find my voice, but the conformist in me wants to give you scientific evidence, which says illness has shown to act as a catalyst for a change for the better. But there is little test tube science here.

But there are so many anecdotal stories from survivors of life-threatening diseases who say their sickness was a gift. Meet two of these inspirational people.

American Barbara Weibel. For 36 years she was driven by the desire to be successful and earn big money. Barbara worked in a variety of corporate jobs from selling real estate, owning a public relations firm, to marketing and advertising. All of these afforded her a comfortable lifestyle. But the money and the variety of work did not make her happy. She wanted more from her life but did not know how. She asked herself 'what brings me joy?' but could find no answers. It was then she became ill. Chronic Lyme disease made her sick for several years but with help from her naturopath, the enforced rest was a time of introspection.

To describe that time in her life she uses the metaphor of a donut, 'a wonderful outer shell with an empty, hollow inside.' She found she could no longer ignore her search for fulfillment. As she recovered from the long debilitating days of sickness, she asked herself again, 'what brings me joy?' The answers came firmly and loudly, 'photography, writing, and travel.'

She promised herself that when she was fully recovered she would find a way of living that gave her that joy. Today she travels permanently, staying in countries for weeks and months to interact with the locals and appreciate their way of life. She posts her photographs and travel articles on her website, aptly named Hole in the Donut Cultural Travel. She earns little money but has never been happier. (holeinthedonut.com).

Neill Duncan is an Australian musician who a few years ago was faced with the cruel decision of having his left arm amputated, or living with the prognosis the sarcoma, a rare and aggressive cancer, could possibly kill him within months. With a wife and four young children, the decision to amputate was a given. The weekend before his operation, his wife organised a party where musicians came from all around the state to celebrate the last two-armed gig for Neill. It was a bittersweet farewell to the musical prowess of a great saxophone player.

Two days later he woke from the operation surrounded by his family and close friends. One of the musicians in his band had Googled 'one-handed saxophone player', and to his excitement found a man in Amsterdam who made one-handed musical instruments for stroke victims and, yes, he could and would make Neill a tenor saxophone.

Two years later the family held another party where Neill amazed all his musician friends with the playing of his custom-made saxophone. A friend filmed the moment and put it on YouTube. Within days, BBC Channel 4 in the UK phoned him and asked him to take part in the 2012 London Paralympics advertisement and to be part of a disabled big swing band, which they were putting together. Oh, and by the way, they were going to film at the Beatles famed Abbey Road studios! Of course, he said yes.

He still gets a lot of pain, (phantom limb pain) but he sees his illness as an absolute blessing: 'it has taken me places I have never dreamed of going, it has shown me love and compassion I could only have imagined.'

Today Aunty G's 'finding the silver lining' has a new handle it is called 'the practice of gratitude.' Universities are studying it, bodies of authors and bloggers are writing about it, and even Oprah is keeping a gratitude journal. And the late Hans Selye—we met in the previous chapter—said: 'The healthiest of all human emotions is gratitude.'

Robert Emmons PhD is the professor of psychology at UC Davis, University of California and author of *Thanks! How the New Science of Gratitude Can Make You Happier*, published in 2015. For over a decade, he has been contributing to the scientific literature on the study of gratitude and well-being. His studies show how the practice of gratitude improves physical and psychological health, and it allows people to form stronger relationships and become more resilient.

I had not been consciously identifying the silver lining as my illness progressed. But daily I knew beyond measure I was grateful to my family—I was the lucky one to be blessed with such support.

Later, as I dabbled daily with my DCPs, I felt an overwhelming sense of gratitude that each of these creative forays gave me so much pleasure and fulfilment. I don't think I said, 'I am grateful for' in those exact words—it was more heart-centred. There was hardly ever a day I did not feel a joyful expectation about the process of creating, and an appreciative satisfaction upon completion.

As the months ticked by, I was vitally aware of the changes taking place, not only physically but also psychologically. It was obvious to all my family I was coping better with the daily challenges of rearing two little ones. It was obvious to me, I felt contentment and a sense of pride in embracing the responsibility of being a single parent. I was no longer needy—I was coming home to me and I was extremely thankful.

Kelly Turner's *New York Times* bestseller book *Radical Remission: Surviving Cancer Against All Odds*, published in 2014, is a must-read for anyone facing a life-threatening disease. Kelly Turner PhD is a charismatic young woman on a mission—writing and producing films and documentaries to discover more about patients' characteristics of recovery from cancer. She too prefers to use the adjective 'radical' when referring to remission rather than 'spontaneous' because for most of the survivors she studies it is not an instant cure, but years of work to beat the odds.

Kelly has analyzed many hundreds of cases of radical remission, and from these, she has identified more than seventy-five factors that survivors reported they used as part of their healing. But in her book, she presents nine of the factors, which were used by almost all of these patients.

These are:

- ♥ Radically changing your diet
- ♥ Taking control of your health
- ♥ Following your intuition
- ♥ Using herbs and supplements
- ♥ Releasing suppressed emotions
- ♥ Increasing positive emotions
- ♥ Embracing social support
- ♥ Deepening your spiritual connection
- ♥ Having strong reasons for living.

I will be comparing Kelly's research factors through the book, but it is so obvious my experiences are in tune with many of these, and the factor 'Increasing positive emotions' equals my take on 'the silver lining.'

But 'silver lining,' or if you prefer—a practice of gratitude—should not be confused with positive thinking.

Norman Vincent Peale was the originator of the theory of positive thinking, and one of America's most loved religious figures. In 1952, his book *The Power of Positive Thinking* was published and for decades it has been a best-seller throughout the world. The book explains how positive thoughts and faith can change you for the better.

In my late teens, I read Dr Peale's book and was impressed. This style of self-transformation has always had great appeal to me and my enthusiasm was high. 'I must be more positive,' I would say, pulling myself up continually. But my dogged determination to be positive could not be sustained, and I found myself once more in the doldrums.

It was only many years later, following a lot of inner work, I saw that saying, 'I must be positive,' negated any possibility of thinking positive. Think about this for a moment - the prefix 'I must' was the giveaway to my psyche—clever little sucker that it is—to recognise if 'I must be' more positive, then the truth is—I am negative!

As we have seen, our stone-age brain is most comfortable being negative. While I used faith/will-power to change and it did work for a while—but then at the first chance, my habit returned to its old and well-waltzed routine once more.

But finding the silver lining, or the science of gratitude, is different—it requires no pressure on oneself to perform, achieve, or succeed. It is a way of being present and appreciating the moment, like clean sun-dried sheets on the bed, a flat-white coffee with good crema, a car that fires the first time on a frosty winter morning, a heart-to-heart with a friend, a garden tended with loving energy, and the list goes on. It is also about a process of reflection. You dig deeper until you find the nitty-gritty of indebtedness and expand on this until you are in touch with it emotionally.

Wise Aunty G's words were a theme for me, searching the many cruel dark days where the silver-lining was almost impossible to detect, but as my energy returned, so did my optimism. In the stillness of this time, I practiced gratitude regularly—I was grateful for the warmth and comfort of my bed, the energy I found to play with my children, to my old sturdy Aga cooker that heated our hot water and warmed the house and slow-cooked the best casserole, and to my family who showed their love unconditionally.

I learned to become grateful to my illness as it was clear it was teaching me. I was blessed. It sharpened me to the inherent goodness of people and the indisputable joy of life.

I love the teachings of Jalaluddin Rumi, the 13th-century Persian poet, theologian and Sufi mystic—such wisdom in his words—I think in this case they even exceed Aunty G's wisdom:

> 'Sorrow prepares you for joy. It violently sweeps everything out of your house, so that new joy can find space to enter. It shakes the yellow leaves from the bough of your heart, so that fresh, green leaves can grow in their place. It pulls up the rotten roots, so that new roots hidden beneath have room to grow. Whatever sorrow shakes from your heart, far better things will take their place.'

Chapter 5

Rejecting the Diagnosis

'If you learn from many wise men who disagree with one another, you will find that there are many wisdoms come out of truth. In the end, you must find truth and define your own wisdom.'
Toba Beta—author of *My Ancestor Was an Ancient Astronaut*

I gave the diagnosis of multiple sclerosis a nodding respect, but at a deeper level, I rejected it. Now, it may well have been I was in denial, but I determined with absolute clarity that my illness was a reflection of my emotional flora and fauna. So, I rejected treatment, and politely refused to join an MS support group.

Today, I see this as essential in my self-healing. Why? Because much of the spiritual soul-searching work I have done throughout my life has led me to the conclusion all human beings are powerful creators, and that with the same mystic power a placebo can heal—by defining myself as the diagnosis, it can equally harm.

I know nothing about physics, but I do get—albeit 'through a glass, darkly'—that we are energy, which attracts like-minded energy. And I see importantly my interpretation of the disease was simply I was unwell, but I would get better with self-care.

I was not associating with a disease label, which could have swallowed me up whole if I had imagined all it meant. Multiple sclerosis: no known cure, incapacity, and an isolated life of chronic illness dependent upon others.

I think if the timing is right and you are in a state of vulnerability, you can easily surrender to an illness. And when you anxiously focus on a disease label or even identify your genetic characteristics as matching those the medical world has determined are risk factors, those thoughts and fears of ill health become a self-fulfilling prophecy.

Today the scientific name for this is 'Nocebo Effect.' Nocebo comes from the Latin nocēre, 'to harm.' The interpretation of nocebo means 'I will be harmful,' and contrasts with placebo, meaning, 'I shall please.'

We all know about placebo—the sugar-coated pill given in double-blind studies, which work as well as the real drug, sham surgeries, which work as well as the real deal, or health improvement arising purely from the caring support of a physician. Recent research has shown there have been 1,500 times more papers written on placebo than on nocebo.

Nocebo controlled studies are relatively few on the scientific horizon, mainly because of the ethical issue arising from inducing pain and misleading volunteers. But the medical research scientists specializing in the placebo and tentative nocebo studies agree there is a need for controlled trials to understand how best to prevent the effects of negative suggestion.

The most obvious nocebo effect is the legendary power of the African witch doctor's 'voodoo' curse that can result in the victim's subsequent death.

Research has found the nocebo effect is a fairly common occurrence. The studies show strongly negative suggestion can induce symptoms of illness. For some volunteers, just being informed of a pill or procedure's potential side effect is enough to bring on real-life symptoms. They found it is important that doctors and nurses choose their words carefully when giving information about possible side effects of drug use, or when advising patients regarding medical procedures. Reframing their expressions in a more positive manner such as 'most people tolerate this procedure well,' is preferable to 'this is going hurt,' or 'you might feel some pain.' Words like pain, sting, burn and hurt especially used more than once have shown to increase the discomfort of the patient.

'Words are the most powerful tool a doctor possesses, but words, like a two-edged sword, can maim as well as heal,' said Dr Bernard Lown, author of several books including *The Lost Art of Healing: Practicing Compassion in Medicine*, published in 1999.

While he is not involved with nocebo studies, Dr Bernard Lown is aware of how an insensitive doctor's manner can impact negatively on a patient.

Dr Lown is my vision of the ideal doctor. He is convinced listening is the physician's greatest tool to uncover the true nature of a disease. He believes doctors today are driven by economic factors and time constraints, and they spend too much time looking at the computer screen rather than face-to-face listening to patients.

Dr Lown tells the story of when he was a young doctor working in Boston, and one of his patients was an 85-year-old spinster—an elegant lady, who for most of her life had an orchestration of aches and ills, but nothing that could be treated.

As she sat before him, her pale face fine-lined with sadness, her eyes lit on some distant spot, he tried to develop a conversation, so he could build her trust. But the elderly lady answered only in monosyllables. After he examined her, his intuition prompted him to ask, 'if you want my help why are so secretive?' The response was immediate. 'No, no, no,' she said, her voice barely a whisper. She turned to him, asking 'you know then?' But not knowing he remained silent.

She told him how as a young nineteen-year-old woman from a reputable upper-class family, she had fallen in love with a married man. Her parents opposed the relationship and warned it would come to a sorry end. When she discovered she was pregnant, she left her family and found work on a farm in the country. It was here that she gave birth alone. And it was here – shockingly—that she threw her new-born down a deep well.

For a lifetime she had carried the guilt of murdering her own child. As Dr Lown documented: 'No amount of self-flagellation diminished the ache, assuaged the sleepless nights, or lighted the crushing weight of guilt. In this fateful examining room, her lifelong search for absolution was now at hand.'

Now, this is the kind of doctor we should all have.

Wait—I can hear you say, 'compassionate physicians are all well and good but if I am desperately sick I want a specialist who is more than a compassionate listener. I want an extraordinary healer.'

For an extraordinary healer, let me introduce you formally to Dr Bernard Lown, Professor Emeritus of Cardiology at the Harvard School of Public Health, Founder of the Lown Institute (formerly known as the Lown Cardiovascular Research Foundation) and the Lown Cardiovascular Centre.

He is known for his research on sudden cardiac death and developing the direct current defibrillator as well as the cardioverter for correcting disordered heart rhythms. To add to these remarkable achievements, I have barely touched on; he is also a Nobel Peace Prize recipient for his work with the International Physicians for the Prevention of Nuclear War (IPPNW).

My brush with nocebo came when I was five months pregnant with Jo, our first child. I had been going for gold with 'morning' sickness, which lasted from the moment I awoke till I went to bed with a bucket beside me. I was continually anxious about the responsibility of being a parent, daily questioning my capabilities about being a mother.

We were enjoying—well Robert was, I was rushing to the toilet—a meal at my parents' house when my father told us in graphic detail about his work colleague who had that day been diagnosed as suffering from Bell's palsy.

'The poor fellow looks as though he has had a stroke; it is

quite dramatic the way the side of his face has dropped. He has to wear an eye-patch, as he can't close his eye at night and has to drink through a straw because if he uses a cup it simply dribbles out of the corner of his mouth. And no, they don't know how he caught it, there is no treatment and they have no idea how long he will have it, they even say he could be like this permanently.'

I remember my nausea abated as I listened with gruesome fascination. All that coming week, I enjoyed a warped victim buzz imagining how awful it would be to have Bell's palsy. I kept rerunning visuals of my drooping mouth, my unblinking eye, and twisted face, and with each replay, I agitated that such an affliction could be permanent. Like any woman in the 1960's I believed looks defined your chances in life and the fear of being struck with a face so contorted it would make me unacceptable to society, consumed me. Shallow I know, but that's the way I was.

A week to the day of my father's account, I awoke to find one side of my face had slipped significantly south and as I drank my cup of tea it dribbled out of the other side of my mouth. It was diagnosed as Bell's palsy, of course, it could well have been the first symptoms of MS, but it mirrored Bell's palsy so perfectly it received this label. I had it for six months.

A coincidence? No. I was then and am still convinced it was the nocebo effect. My emotional and physical stressors created the right environment for my mind to secure the Bell's palsy story as my own.

So, was it a coincidence multiple sclerosis mirrored all of my limiting beliefs? Well, if you were designing an illness to reflect those stories of worthlessness, uselessness, incapability, not being enough and powerlessness, then MS would be a worthy candidate. My body, plagued by weakness and paralysis for this intense period of the disease was incapable and powerless. Bedridden and unable to manage my children and home, I was indeed not enough.

Did my fertile imagination with its constant repetition of my dark-side characteristics of victim-hood create this Dickensian melodrama?

How ridiculous is this question, I think, when as a child I spent most of my childhood playing with an imaginary friend.

I see it is more than possible a seed can easily take root as we tick the boxes of emotional and physical feelings of distress. I have come to the conclusion that what I didn't know had no opportunity to hurt me.

Most people, when faced with an illness, seek answers. The initial step is pursuing a second opinion and reviewing all the conventional medical options before possibly exploring alternative healing methods. And with one scroll of the internet, people can find comprehensive and up-to-date information on their disease—overwhelming amounts of data—reports that substantiate trials, offer risk percentages, and studies that tell them definitively what they should and should not be doing or eating.

Contemporary society is in love with data; almost every other day a new piece of research is given credence by the media. Coffee has escalated from being the assassin to a miracle preventative. Sugar—sweet and deadly, lethal to dental caries—from being another carbohydrate and then to pure unadulterated toxin for our body. Red wine has held steady as being good for us while new evidence shows staying out of the sun entirely can increase cancer risks; or taking fish oil, exercising, and doing puzzles doesn't help fend off Alzheimer's disease.

We check in with what appeals to us from this onslaught of research filling our screens print and social media and gloss over at what we see as ridiculous.

But most of us take it as gospel when the medical world speaks—medical headlines always catch our attention. Extensive research shows how certain types of people are at higher risk of certain diseases. Medical websites and health publications endorse the messages – for example: 'Substantial data has been analysed to show people who internalise anger are more likely to succumb to cancer.' Or 'Type A people, competitive, who strive towards goals with little joy in their achievements are more than likely to suffer heart disease.'

Of course, all this research data, including the risk factors of genetics, age, poor diet, and smoking, is collected with the best intention to warn and give notice if you are this type of personality and you have ticked the boxes of risk factors, you Sir or Madam; unless you take action, are the ideal candidate for a terminal disease.

John P A Ioannidis a Professor of Health Research and Policy at Stanford School of Medicine is recognised as one of the world's foremost experts on the credibility of medical research. Heading up a team of scientific medical researchers whose work is to sift through the myriad of published papers and reports to determine whether the outcomes are without bias, are not misleading, exaggerated or flawed.

The bad news is Professor Ioannidis believes up to 90% of the published material doctors rely on is flawed. (Reference: PLoS Medicine paper on 'Why Most Published Research Findings are False.' 2005—John P A Ioannidis, Professor of Health Research and Policy at Stanford School of Medicine)

Professor Ioannidis is not a renegade or a maverick out to get the drug companies or medical researchers. On the contrary, he is widely respected by the medical world and in demand for his work. He sees clearly the objectivity of any medical research is questionable, that is, without bias.

How the heck, you ask, can this happen, when we know these studies are rigorous and ruthlessly controlled? But is it so surprising when these studies are undertaken by mortals, not robots, and people, however well qualified, disciplined or intentioned, have been found to be affected by their research agendas, whether knowingly or unconsciously?

Because of the variables and human factors involved, it is difficult to set up a study, which is not biased, Professor Ioannidis reports. He has found the studies are often driven by the need to maintain research funding adding pressure on researchers to reach the desired results. For instance, researchers may cherry-pick positive trials and discount the negative, a drug company may set up a study comparing their new drug to a previous one that is inferior, or researchers may simply ask questions, which are biased, whether intentionally or unconsciously. From there it is easy to manipulate the data to get the result they believe is conclusively right.

Of course, this bias may happen with any sourced data. An illustration of how a question can give you a solid chance of only one result occurred in Australia in 1999 when the government of the day held a referendum to ask whether the Constitution of Australia should be amended to become a republic.

For many years, there had been an enthusiastic push for Australia to cut the apron strings with the United Kingdom. At the time of the referendum, it was widely thought most people would vote in favour of Australia becoming a republic.

Instead of a straightforward question being asked— whether you were for or against Australia becoming a republic—the question given to voters was: 'Should Australia become a republic with a President appointed by Parliament?' This question was not only contrary to what the nation expected, but also the logistics of how we would set up a Republic had not been explored in depth. Consequently, the option 'with a President appointed by Parliament' with no prior consultation with the public, meant that the referendum was soundly defeated.

Both my parents died at the age of 63, too young. My father had severe heart disease, and he was one of the first in Britain to have open-heart surgery. My mother died of cancer. Only one of my grandparents was alive when I was born, but four all died early from either cancer or cardiovascular disease. As I geared up to my sixth decade, I firmly believed in the expert knowledge provided at the time by the medical world—meant that I was, genetically, history. My inherited genes all pointed to an early death. I was anxious, convinced I was either going to drop dead from heart disease or cancer by the time

I reached 63. Today I am testament that not all-conclusive evidence is right.

One thing I have learned in life is there is no definitive knowledge—the world around us is continually evolving, as does our understanding of science. Yesterday coffee was the villain—today the hero in the fight against cancer. Yesterday, margarine was the hero—today the villain. In WWI, people were encouraged to smoke—'good for the nerves'—doctors said to patients, as they too puffed away in their surgeries. Little did they know...but history should teach us profiling personality types and risk factors are tenuous. What we know now may be different in a decade's time. One size does NOT fit all!

This becomes apparent when you hear the story about a compelling study coming out of Scotland recently. Since the 1950s, they have had a growth rate of incidents of coronary heart disease, especially in the younger generation; in fact, they had the highest rate in Europe. The first flush of assumption—based on what the medical world identifies as proven risk factors—presumed that the culprit was smoking, drinking, and a heavily laden saturated fat diet.

But as the Chief Medical Officer of Scotland Sir Harry Burns and his team investigated more thoroughly, they found the decline of heavy industry was the key factor, which led them to the understanding it was social inequality that drove the problem. The known risk factors for booze, smoking, and the all-time Scottish favourite of deep fried battered Mars Bars were not the primary cause.

What became apparent was the annihilating effect of the closure of the steel industry on the population's psyche. Workers were given a financial hand-out, but no skill retraining, and no opportunity for work. People felt powerless. Crime, drug taking, and suicide increased.

The feeling of hopelessness and powerlessness passed from one generation to the next, as did the incidents of diabetes, stroke and cardiovascular disease.

Sir Harry Burns, now Professor of Global Public Health at Strathclyde University, says that prevention does not lie in the routine medical pre-emptive measures of drugs, diet, and exercise, but is pushing to understand more fully the effects of social inequality in families.

Sir Harry is an advocate of Aaron Antonovsky, an American-Israeli medical sociologist, and his investigations into the origins of health—which Antonovsky termed salutogenesis (origins: Latin salus—health and Greek genesis—creation, generation), as contrasted with the normal medical science's investigations into the causes of disease (pathogenesis from the Greek—pathos suffering/ill health and genesis origin, creation, generation).

In the 1970s Antonovsky was conducting a routine health study of menopausal Israeli women—some of whom had lived through the hell of concentration camps of World War II. He had expected this group of Holocaust survivors would be emotionally and physically affected by their ordeal—but what he found amazed him. While the majority of these women suffered ongoing health issues and dysfunctional lives, there were a few who not only had good health, but their lives appeared to be well-balanced and successful. More than intrigued, he examined these successful survivors' lives more intensely and found what he believed was a common denominator. This commonality allowed these women to not only cope with the horrors of their childhood but to be able to live healthy and fulfilling lives. It became evident to him the way people view their life has a positive influence on how they handle stressors that affect their health.

From this work, he introduced his Salutogenic Theory 'Sense of Coherence in 1979', to explain to the world why some people become ill under stress, while others stay healthy.

He defined the sense of coherence (SOC) as a deep-seated feeling of confidence—a sense of knowing one's environment is predictable, that things will work out as well as can reasonably be expected, obstacles in life are manageable, and a conviction that there is a meaningful purpose to one's life.

I like his style of research and conclusions, which is the same as all of the previous scientists I have quoted. I acknowledge I am biased in choosing research that suits my purpose. This and previous research falls neatly in line with my thinking my ill health emanated from my conscious and unconscious mind.

From Antonovsky's work, I see that despite my chaotic childhood, somehow I achieved this sense of coherence, which worked so strongly in my favour—a strong conviction all would be well, knowing my family would support me, and I had the most meaningful purpose of two children who needed me to be whole.

Sadly, Antonovsky, at the age of 71, contracted leukemia and died within weeks of being diagnosed. One report of his death used the words 'he was struck down with a terminal illness,' and I am sure it would have had Antonovsky turning in his grave—he never saw disease as a thief in the continuum of health.

> 'We are coming to understand health not as the absence of disease, but rather as the process by which individuals maintain their sense of coherence (i.e. sense that life is comprehensible, manageable, and meaningful) and ability to function in the face of changes in themselves and their relationships with their environment.' *Unravelling the Mystery of Health. How People Manage Stress and Stay Well*, Aaron Antonovsky, published in 1987.

There are people whose lives are smitten with a chronic disease, and for some, it may well be their spirit's chosen path to enlightenment. My friend Patty, who I met on a cruise in the Pacific, is one of these.

Patty, a registered nurse is a pretty woman with glowing skin, who has a ready smile to greet all. The only clues that Patty suffered from a rare and chronic gastro-intestinal life-threatening disorder were at dinner when she navigated the menu so cautiously—her limited choices dependent on her ongoing health. These disorders have held her captive for nigh on 20 years. Her sickness is so complex it took 10 years of diligent seeking to receive a complete diagnosis. This diagnosis she said was vital in the pathway to accurate treatment, and crucially gave her the empowerment of self-managing this chronic illness.

I quote from her correspondence to me:

'When my two gastro-intestinal disorders became much worse in the early 90's, I took a two-year leave of absence from work and traveled around the country seeking additional medical information and exploring non-traditional treatments. I felt a sense of empowerment that I was taking hold of my situation and not just being a victim. I think this feeling of being empowered was extremely important. In my travels, I became aware of the profound relationship between mind and body, and the damaging effect of chronic stress if not handled appropriately. I had acupuncture, which I found very helpful, had further diagnostic testing which revealed another gastro-intestinal issue that hadn't been diagnosed and was important to identify. I went to a pain clinic, learned mindfulness meditation, listened to relaxation tapes, tried herbal supplements as well as my medications, tried to learn self-hypnosis (this was tough to master) and learned how diet affected my disease. I reached a point of acceptance of my illness, rather than continuing to fight it, and always worry about what was around the corner. It was so important to learn that flare-ups I suffered were significantly affected by anxiety, and stress.'

Today Patty copes with these disorders through diet, stress management and the practice of mindfulness. She enjoys every bite of food that she is able to digest. She travels widely with her husband, seeing new places, meeting new friends. You could well say she sucks the very marrow out of life.

We are all different. For Patty, the accurate diagnosis allowed her to accept and manage her chronic condition. My path to recovery was dependent that the diagnosis did not define me; if I had believed the diagnosis of MS I believe it would have had its execrable way with me.

Robert Rabbin is a survivor of stage 4, non-small-cell lung

cancer, who was originally given nine months to live, over five years ago. Robert had previously practiced meditation for a decade and when he received an intuitive message—which he believed emanated from the spirit of his long-dead meditation teacher, Swami Muktananda—it changed the way he viewed his cancer. 'Robert, don't say you have cancer; if you must say something, just say that you are holding the space for cancer to visit you temporarily.' *Radical Remission: Surviving Cancer Against All Odds*, Kelly Turner PhD, published in 2014.

I hear you—we need to know what we are dealing with, and yes, of course, it would be medical anarchy if we did not. We need specialists whose work and expertise lies solely within a specific disease. But I still say, defining ourselves as a diagnosis, for a many of us, is like baiting the hook and casting in the shallows, where our minds like to feed. I must say Swami Muktananda's message has great appeal: 'holding the space,' sounds good to me.

Chapter 6

Stillness and Surrender

*'In My Secret Life
I saw you this morning,
you were moving so fast.
Can't seem to loosen my grip
On the past.
And I miss you so much,
there's no one in sight.
And we're still making love
In my secret life.
I smile when I am angry,
I cheat and I lie,
I do what I have to do
to get by,
In my secret life.'*

Leonard Cohen—Singer, Songwriter, Musician, Poet, Novelist

In World War 1, so many young men were lost it was hard to keep up with the mourning standards imposed in the

Victorian era. Society moved away from the heavy melancholia of the Victorian way of mourning with its formal observance of pre-funeral rituals, black crape bows on the front door, and the wearing of black mourning clothes for two years by the immediate family of the deceased.

Fifty years ago, the way society dealt with death and funerals was different from today. As a gleaming black hearse passed through the streets, men would remove their hat or cap and bow their heads. Black armbands as a symbol of mourning, de rigueur in Victorian days, were still a common sight, and people wore black to funerals. Contrary to present day with people being open about their feelings and can be seen to share their grief on social media posts, in the 50s and 60s people studiously avoided talking of death. People would cross the street to avoid talking with the bereaved because they were not sure of saying the 'right' thing.

Today's vogue expression 'closure' has again re-defined the way our society looks at bereavement. We have packaged it. 'Closure' is interpreted as a pivotal step in grief management. It is a platitude that echoes community sentiments that 'once the bereaved have 'closure' they are free to get on with the 'business of grief.'"

To those who haven't suffered a personal loss, the 'business of grief,' is viewed very differently from those who are grieving. It is human nature to want to find a fix, a cure for someone's grief. Clichés roll off our well-intentioned tongues like 'God never gives you more than you can handle,' 'time heals all wounds,' and with the presumption grief is finite this provides the latitude to intervene with ... 'it's time to put it behind you and move on.'

Those in the throes of grief are on a different page. 'Closure' is a myth and is insulting to those who are grieving. There is no closure. Grief does not end. But in time, the rawness of the dreadful gaping wound lessens and the bereaved learn to live with their loss and create a new life around it. But the truth is they will never be the same again.

Through all my experience and subsequent research, the one thing that strikes me most is the vital importance of rituals in the healing process of grief.

I have grieved many times in my life. I have mourned the loss of my identity as a mother and carer as my children left home. I have mourned the loss of my parents who died too young. I have mourned for my green and gentle birthplace as I tackled a new country with light so bright it hurts the eyes, bush-fires, and flash-floods. I have mourned the loss of my working identity as I transitioned to retirement. It is the price of living and loving, but from these tears, with time, came joyful memories sacred to me.

Why then did the harrowing legacy of my grief of losing Robert complicate me for so long? I only knew him for five years, of which I was married for just a week less than two years. I compare this with my healthier grief process upon the loss of my parents whom I loved equally and were in my life until my mid-thirties.

The main difference was that his death was not a natural part of life—it was unpredicted and catastrophic. The ripple effect of this complex grief widened ever more to affect his children as they grew.

My father identified Robert's badly disfigured body. 'Not a job for a woman,' he said. My sister-in-law said, 'I will plan the funeral.' There was no plan or ceremony to scatter his ashes, as these were collected from the crematorium by my sister-in-law and taken back to Australia to be buried under a rose bush at his family's place of worship. Trauma bound me so fiercely I did not query or understand the spiritual value of these vital markers and rituals of death and mourning.

Maybe I would have found some resolution to my chaotic grief pattern if I had viewed his body, being able to kiss him a final time, and sit quietly beside his body asking him to forgive me for not accepting him unconditionally and to let him go with love. If I had played an active role in planning his funeral, putting flowers and his favourite things in his coffin, choosing the music, the eulogises, and poetry. Or if I had insisted on retaining some of his ashes to be buried in our favourite parkland where I could have had a sacred retreat to visit and spend time with my memories. But I didn't, and my grief was comprised, complicated, and unresolved.

Today I see I was suffering from a grieving complication called 'ambiguous loss.'

Ambiguous loss (AL) is a term coined by American researcher and author Dr Pauline Boss in the 1970s. *Ambiguous Loss: Learning to Live with Unresolved Grief*, published in 1999.

In my correspondence with Dr Boss, she explained that ambiguous loss is a complicated loss that leads to a type of complicated grief.

AL or 'a type of complicated grief,' the grief process is frozen and generates feelings of helplessness; hopelessness, anxiety and guilt, and when it comes to making decisions about life the bereaved feel stuck, paralysed, and overwhelmed.

The most catastrophic AL comes from events where there is not a body to mourn such as servicemen lost in action, airline crashes and people lost at sea. It also strikes families where a child is abducted, who live all their lives not knowing whether their child is alive or dead, or families learning to live with the ravages of dementia or Alzheimer Disease that leaves just a shell of the person.

One can only imagine the resilience of these people as they learn to live with this irresolvable quandary.

But AL is not limited to these extreme situations. There are other events such as when a child loses a parent to divorce, mothers who give up their child for adoption, or adopted children, people who are separated from their loved ones by immigration or when a former lover or spouse is still very much missed.

Dr Boss said, 'Without comprehension, they can't make sense of their situation to cope. Without meaning, they can't find hope to help them move forward with their lives. They are simply stuck.'

So clearly, I see the ongoing consequences of my truth of intellectually knowing but emotionally unable to grasp the finality of Robert's death.

I was not alone struggling with this complicated grief. Jo, thirteen months, and Neil two weeks old at the time of Robert's death were protected, as best my family and I could from the pain and turmoil of that time, but with the passing of the years, you could see how his death impacted on all the family. Jo and Neil suffered the double whammy of loss of their father and an emotional absence of their mother in this important time of their lives. I was physically there doing all that a mother should, but I was emotionally absent.

In Jo and Neil's teenage years we stood silently by the rose bush that marked where their father's ashes were buried in the church grounds on his anniversary and paid homage. But it was in their early fifties that Jo and Neil and their families found more meaningful solace when they held their own memorial service for their father—symbolically held at the end of a grassy airport runway.

Unresolved grief is a corroding deep-seated sorrow, affecting all who live through it, and continues on through the generations.

To put this into context, frequently we see in the media today stories of families displaying heartfelt emotions as they pay their respects at the faraway lands of soldiers who were lost in World War 1 or World War 11. We hear the stories of deep sorrow that bound and paralysed these families for generations. Often these people's relative was never known to them, are astonished at the depth of their feelings as they take this journey into the past to find the gravesites of the fallen.

Dr Boss's work shows that by sharing the loss with a counselor or peer group it can lessen the effects of this complicated grief, as does taking control of your life by some activity such as writing, playing a musical instrument, and so on. It is important to surround yourself with people who give you unconditional support and love. It is important to understand that you are not to blame for 'not getting over the grief' and recognise that other family members may feel the same, accepting that closure may never happen. And finally, her research shows the benefits of finding the greater good in life to generate new hope.

At the time of Robert's death, there was no counseling, no peer group to share my angst with but I had a family that supported me and listened to me without judgment. Fifty years later I understand I was not to blame for the messiness of grief that was mine for so long. And I see that 'new hope' was engendered by my daily creative projects, which healed me in so many ways.

The world lost the legendary Leonard Cohen in 2016. He was born in Montreal in 1934, into a middle-class Jewish family. From his youth, he wrote poetry and novels through to his middle years. His first volume of poetry was published at the age of twenty-two and it won him a small grant to travel to Europe. He fell in love with the Greek Island of Hydra—here he bought a house, it had no electricity or running water—and lived and wrote on the island off and on for nearly a decade. It wasn't until his early thirties he tried his talents at songwriting. Amongst the many songs he wrote was the haunting *Hallelujah*—his recording of it slipped under the mainstream radar but well and truly has been brought back to our consciousness by other recording stars – I am thinking of another Canadian K D Lang who took this glorious song to a new level.

In the 1990's Leonard Cohen stole away from the material world and joined a Zen Buddhist Centre in California where he took a vow of silence, became an ordained Zen monk and remained there for five years. He said he wasn't looking for a new religion, Judaism had served him well, but he felt he needed to address a great sense of disorder in his life. It was here he practiced the task of going 'nowhere.' The idea behind it was choosing to be still long enough to turn inward.

In his book, *The Art of Stillness: Adventures of Going Nowhere*, published in 2014, Pico Iyer, travel writer and essayist interviewed Cohen about the philosophy of going 'nowhere.' Cohen's answer was 'it isn't about turning your back on the world; it's about stepping away now and then so that you can see the world clearly and love it more deeply.'

Florence Nightingale, social reformer and founder of modern nursing, held a strong conviction. 'That quiet is a part of care, as essential for patients as medication or sanitation.'

It seems silence or quietness boosts our creativity, makes us more content, and stimulates our search for profound meaning in our lives.

In 2006, Dr Luciano Bernardi of the University of Pavia, Italy, conducted a study of the effects of music on our cardio and respiratory health. Luciano and his team studied two-dozen test subjects who listened to a random series of six two-minute musical tracks. Bernardi found music did stimulate changes in the body, but the most interesting and surprising result came when they looked at the two-minute silent tracks, which interspersed the music.

Here it was seen that silence was far more relaxing than 'relaxing' music. It was shown it reduced the activity of the sympathetic nervous system, which triggers the fight-or-flight syndrome. (2006 Study published in the journal *Heart*.)

In 2013 researcher Dr Imke Kirste found that mice subjected to two hours of silence per day showed growth of new cells in the hippocampus, the region of the brain which leads to improved learning and memory. These cells, in turn, appeared to become functioning neurons. In lay terms, silence can literally grow your brain, which is extremely good news for aging brains! (2013 study, published in journal 'Brain, Structure and Function.')

So, if periods of quiet can be seen to be so effective as growing the brain then surely, I hypothesise, it must be effective for healing our ills.

In the down-and-out stage of my sickness, I had no choice, as there was no more fight left in me. I had to turn inwards, not always consciously, but the quiet of my bedroom became my Zen sanctuary.

This quiet, this time of introspection, this turning inwards during those long months, I see now was a form of a practice of meditation. Even as I became a little stronger with each passing week, I was able to do a few chores before climbing back into bed and once again sink deep into my comfortable bed, my mind only focused on my breathing—breath in, breath out—and with each breath relaxing more and more deeply. During this hibernating period, my mind was free of the constant barrage of guilt. I had done what I had to do to get my life back on track before the illness bit hard. I knew my children were receiving the best of care, and it was up to me to rest and grow stronger.

Fortunately, I was born into a real family who went through the high and hard times together. My mother and my sister particularly gave me not only the physical support of day-to-day care of my children but also the emotional freedom of supporting my choice of rejecting conventional treatment. Without this support, God knows how it would have panned out.

'Embracing social support' is one of the nine key factors researcher Kelly Turner, (*Radical Remission: Surviving Cancer Against All Odds,* published in 2014) found in common with over a 1000 people who experienced radical healing. As was 'Deepening your spiritual connection,' which I was experiencing during the quiet meditative state of my time out.

Meditation does not fare well in scientific studies, mainly because of the poor design and quality of trials. Scientists at the John Hopkins University in Baltimore, Maryland USA reviewed 19,000 meditation studies, and only 3% (47) of these met their criteria. They could only conclude, from this small sample range, of the effectiveness of meditation was 'moderate.' At the same time, the John Hopkins' researchers challenged scientists to produce better quality trials. But they knew that meditation might provide a range of lifestyle benefits that are difficult to measure.

Anecdotally, there is a wealth of evidence out there to tell of the effectiveness of meditation in healing—not only healing depression and anxiety—but is often used as an adjunct to other healing methodologies.

Ian Gawler and his wife Dr Ruth Gawler provide retreats and training in meditation and yoga in Australia and New Zealand. Ian's message: 'Meditation is the single most powerful tool to aid recovery from disease and lead a life of maximum health.'

Ian Gawler was a veterinarian and promising athlete when in 1957, he had his right leg amputated due to bone cancer. Cancer reappeared later that year, and his future looked desperately bleak but using a wide range of treatment methods and self-help options he miraculously survived. Since then, he has become a leader and advocate of meditation, and mind-body techniques in the Western world. As the 20th century idiom says, 'he talks the talk and walks the walk.' His life work with his wife, is now committed to helping others as they weather through a serious illness.

You can read his inspirational biographical story in Guy Allenby's book, *Ian Gawler: The Dragon's Blessing*, published in 2008.

I define surrender, or you may prefer the term 'letting go,' as the emotional point when you no longer resist or are in conflict with the trauma or disease, and you allow yourself to be at one with it.

Leonard Cohen said it perfectly 'if you don't become the ocean, you'll be seasick every day.'

The longer I live, the more I am convinced that if you can get out of its way, the body knows how to heal itself. And when I was Rip Van Winkle lying on a dreamless bed, it was able to do what it needed to mend me.

'I said to my soul, be still and wait without hope, for hope would be hope for the wrong thing; wait without love, for love would be love of the wrong thing; there is yet faith, but the faith and the love are all in the waiting. Wait without thought, for you are not ready for thought: So the darkness shall be the light, and the stillness the dancing.'

T.S. Eliot –Poet and Nobel Prize Winner for Literature 1948

Chapter 7

Trusting and Acting Upon My Intuition

'The doctor of the future will be oneself.'
Albert Schweitzer—Theologian, Musician, Philosopher, Physician

'I knew I should—or shouldn't—have done that! I knew it! I told myself this would happen!' How many times have we all said that? The pianissimo voice gives us the insistent tightening of the gut message; only to be discounted by what we believe is logical and constructive thinking.

Today we live in a world dominated by procedures, methodology, measures, and standards, which stifle our imagination and spontaneity. It is hard to recognise the little inner voice of wisdom and safekeeping—our intuition.

So, let's introduce this chapter with quotes from twentieth

and twenty-first- century intellectual heroes:

Albert Einstein, Nobel prize winner for physics and arguably the greatest scientist of our time, was a staunch advocate for intuition, and amongst several of his quotes about intuition said: 'The intuitive mind is a sacred gift and the rational mind is a faithful servant. We have created a society that honours the servant and has forgotten the gift.'

Jonas Salk is the man who saved generations from polio, and is another of the twentieth century's most respected scientists, he said: 'It is always with excitement that I wake up in the morning wondering what my intuition will toss up to me, like gifts from the sea. I work with it and rely on it. It's my partner.'

Richard Branson, the entrepreneur extraordinaire, said: 'I have always done everything by intuition and gut feeling, and almost never used accountants to decide if I should start a new business.'

Steve Jobs, co-founder of Apple Computers, said upon returning from a visit to India: 'The people in the Indian countryside don't use their intellect like we do, they use their intuition instead, and their intuition is far more developed than in the rest of the world... Intuition is a very powerful thing, more powerful than intellect, in my opinion.' *Steve Jobs* —Walter Isaacson, published in 2011.

What is intuition? Albert Einstein defined it as: 'Intuition is nothing but the outcome of earlier intellectual experience.' Malcolm Gladwell who wrote the best-seller *Blink: The Power of Thinking Without Thinking* published in 2005, agrees intuition is all about the brain rapidly slicing empirical experience and knowledge to prompt—'blink'—the intuitive message.

Even today, with good scientific evidence of the validity

of intuition, many people still view it with suspicion and opt to use research and data to make a decision—in other words, sharpen your pencil to write a list of pros and cons. But science now shows a 'gut decision,' 'intuition,' or 'hunch' is not something fanciful—it is as Einstein said based on a depth of experience that stems from our unconscious.

Gut feelings come from deep in the brain in a region called the insula. Evidence from MRI scans shows that the insula is the cornerstone or wellspring of social emotions—from love, lust, pain, shame, addiction, craving, the enjoyment of music, and the appreciation of wine.

Gerd Gigerenzer is director of the Center for Adaptive Behavior and Cognition at the Max Planck Institute for Human Development in Berlin and is one of the leading researchers in the field of human decision-making. He is the author of *Gut Feelings: The Intelligence of the Unconscious*, published in 2008.

Gigerenzer says we should trust our intuition as it can be demonstrated our 'gut feelings' are the result of unconscious mental processes.

He says: 'Gut feelings are tools for an uncertain world. They're not caprice. They are not a sixth sense or God's voice. They are based on lots of experience, an unconscious form of intelligence.'

His work has shown we use heuristics—definition: rules of thumb—which we derive from our environment, and prior experiences when using our intuition. He sees heuristics as tools that deal with uncertainty.

His work has lead him to conclude 'less is more,' meaning that you can effectively come to a decision with less research and less data, by relying on your own tried and tested rules of thumb.

I cannot do justice to this man's vital work—it is way above my batting average—and speaking of sport, he explains splendidly how fielders, be it cricket or baseball can seem to pluck the most unlikely catch from the air. Is it because they do complicated calculations to pace themselves to be in the right spot at the right moment? No, says Gigerenzer it is because they—either consciously or unconsciously—follow simple heuristics and these are to simply fix their gaze on the ball, and maintain the angle, as they run in the direction of the ball.

Now haven't we always known it—how many times did we hear the coach in sports yell? 'Just keep your eye on the ball, just keep your eye on the ball.'

To help me understand heuristics—rules of thumbs a little more—I looked more closely at my first attempt at doing an intuitive reading for other people.

A decade ago I was attending a 'Develop Your Intuition Workshop.' The exercise given to us was to access our intuition and give people, whom we had never met before, whatever our intuition offered.

I was sweaty-palm nervous, but the first two women I found relatively easy to read. I think my readings were based on the total package of the individual—clothes, hair, way of phrasing their words, facial and hand gestures. So, I could understand how I would have used simple heuristics based on my recognition and biases of past experiences of a certain profile of people with an interest in self-development, augmented with awareness of their posture and body language

A JOURNEY OF CREATIVE HEALING

and being empathetic to their responses. While some of the reading felt it was smart conscious guessing, much of it flowed on from what was obvious to me.

The last person I had to read was a man who was conservatively dressed and restrained in his manner, his face and clothes giving nothing away. I followed the instructions of relaxing, letting my anxieties—like clouds in the sky—float on by when an image popped into my head of black patent dancing shoes. Unlike the women before, there were no obvious conscious clues at all. At the time, my neocortex said 'ridiculous,' but when it came time to talk, I had nothing to run with save the black patent shoes. As I spoke, one of the black patent shoes in the image fell away and I had a sense of knowing, apart from a love of ballroom dancing, this man had recently suffered a broken relationship. As I talked, my hunches simply pushed images into my mind, which were obvious and easy to interpret. So why did the dancing shoes land as a clear symbol in my brain? Maybe at an unconscious level I saw how he held his head, moved his shoulders, and this reminded me of a ballroom dancer, but this is pure supposition. My recently divorced champion ballroom dancer was as gobsmacked as I was. Both of us said 'wow where did that come from? '

> 'There comes a leap in consciousness—call it intuition or what you will—when the solution comes to you and you don't know how or why ... The truly valuable thing is the intuition.' **Albert Einstein.**

Again, I turn to Kelly Turner, author, and founder of the Radical Remission Project. In her book *Radical Remission:*

Surviving Cancer Against All Odds' she identifies key factors that were consistently reported in the remission cases she examined. It is remarkable out of a thousand cases she found seventy-five different factors—but of this number, nine consistently surfaced.

In an interview, Turner was asked about one of these key factors – 'Following Your Intuition.' She said this factor was a surprise, as she did not think intuition would come up in every single interview she conducted, but it did. But, she asserted, it makes sense when people are in life-threatening situations, they hear their intuitive voice so strongly.

Intuition can come in many ways. It may come as a soft voice in your head, or an image in a dream, as you journal, or simply through a synchronistic link with another. And as can be seen from Turner's studies, when life is threatened, the voice is insistent.

As it was, in my case my intuition came like a zap to the brain when I watched my children play and saw so clearly my daughter Jo playing the role of the nurturer. Of course, kids do that—role-play being Mum or Dad with other children. But the impact of that moment of realization, I had not been there emotionally for my children, could not be dismissed by logic. I was instantly aware of my heartfelt desire to change my life.

My second epiphany was equally powerful a few months later, in my lounge on an early spring morning. The gas fire blue flames leaped and spluttered, as I settled myself on the settee to listen to one of my favourite classical recordings Rimsky Korsakov Scheherazade. The music echoed my emotions—or I should say I echoed the emotion of music. I sank lower into the couch with the opening bars of the power of the brass instruments, followed by the sweetness of the flutes and piccolos, before the exquisite solo violin filled my heart.

As the music came to an end, a voice spoke in my head. It was clear and strong. I was left in no doubt of its authenticity. 'You are right not to give credence to the diagnosis of your illness. Your body is simply creating symptoms that mirror your deepest fear of being alone and of not being capable to shoulder the burden of the responsibility of raising two children on your own.'

I stood up slowly…everything was clear and bright. Through the window, the sunrays fanned across the clouds like some Renaissance painting. It was surreal. Again, I heard my intuitive voice: 'I need to put my focus on being creative. Yes, that's it, a creative project. I need to create something new each day. It doesn't matter what—I need to focus on the planning and joy of creativity.'

I think my unconscious intelligence was offering up the childhood pleasure of simple creative enterprises, knowing these daily missions would give me joy, focus, and purpose. Being so engaged, it would assuage my fears of living a solitary life without a partner, and with each successful completion of a daily creative project, it would help build emotional resilience to face my responsibilities.

Before you doubt—was that not a fair description of the end result of my commitment to a daily creative practice?

Like the cancer survivors in Kelly Turner's book, not once did I question it—the drama of the lounge room first message, akin to Moses meeting God on Mount Sinai, and then the practical second message a few minutes later. I did not spend time analyzing either message. I was alive with creative energy.

I have learned intuition is simply an amazing gift. No matter whether you think the message you receive is crazy or worse if you trust it and act upon it, you find the intuitive message will guide you to what is best.

This is how I was taught to access my intuition:

- Find a quiet area of your home, or even better in nature—somewhere where you will not be disturbed.

- Sit quietly, silently contemplating what is going on for you in your life.

- Acknowledge your busy mind, your body feeling stressed, and the anxiety you may have surrounding your ability to access your intuition. As you acknowledge the tensions, you will slowly relax.

- Draw an imaginary circle around you. The circle is a traditional symbol of wholeness, infinity, eternity.

- Relaxed and sitting comfortably within your protective circle, set your intention to receive an answer to a question.

- Make a choice to 'go into innocence.' This feeling of innocence can be prompted with a visualization of a moment in nature, a glimpse of your pet, a remembrance of the wonder of holding a newborn baby, etc. It can be anything you remember as a pure moment of joy and wonder. (I have a picture of me at four years old trying to ride an oversized tricycle; the joy on my face takes me straight into that feeling of innocence and bliss).

- Then pose your question again.

- ♥ The answer can come in many ways. It might be a direct message, or it can be a symbol, image or written phrase. If you receive a symbol or image, you will need to interpret it. Ask yourself, what is obvious about it? (Going back to the black patent shoes, it was obvious to me these were ballroom dancing shoes—so he must be a dancer, in my mind, they were high gloss shiny, and shine = sparkle = star-quality = champion ballroom dancer. When one shoe dropped away abruptly, it was obvious it was a metaphor for a partnership—once there were two, now only one).

Meditation gives the most powerful intuitive response, and combined with the technique above, will unfailingly deliver the answer. Now, of course, the trick is to trust what you receive.

Reading about others intuitive moments in Kelly Turner's book *Radical Remission: Surviving Cancer Against All Odds*, I was struck by the similarities of other's life-changing intuitive experiences. One of these patients, Susan, was given the terrible news her cancer was stage four, and without immediate surgery, radiation and chemotherapy, she would not live the year out. She was shocked, and trying to process all her specialist was saying to her when she heard an insistent voice in her head saying, 'Not that way, not this time,' and she left the doctor's office without explanation. She said the voice made her feel she had been: 'Taken care of by something larger.' She successfully took her own alternative health route to wellness.

Listening and acting upon my intuition was key in my road to recovery, both physically and spiritually.

Is intuition simply the result of accumulative experiences and knowledge the brain dips into, and voila up comes the answer? While I acknowledge the scientific findings that say it is the unconscious delivering an answer based on our empirical experience, my heart tells me there is something more and it may well be as Susan said, one of being 'taken care of by something larger.'

Chapter 8

Focusing on my Daily Creative Projects

What drains your spirit drains your body.

What fuels your spirit fuels your body.
Caroline Myss—Medical Intuitive and Pioneer of Energy Healing

It was early afternoon and the children were asleep. The kitchen was quiet, apart from the Aga making odd hissing noises as the flames licked the coke in the old fuel stove. I sat on the green vinyl bench seat in the corner breakfast nook with its faux timber Formica bench. My cup of tea turned cold as I dashed notes onto my writing pad for my next DCP. (Reminder: DCP is an acronym for daily creative projects.) I was making plans for new seat covers for my old tired looking dining room chairs. I had purchased the walnut timber dining setting second hand, and while the chairs were in decent condition, the fabric of the seats was faded and shiny. My notes gained momentum:

Library Research (No internet in the 1960s)

How to recover chairs
Amount of material?
Special tools?
Need to measure chairs
Where to shop for fabric? Do I need special material?

The children and I had already completed the day's DCP. In the morning I had taken the children on a new adventure to a forest, where we had morning tea of homemade scones with jam and cream sitting on a blanket in a wooded clearing, amidst the bounty of an early autumn day. Later the children ran wild, their sticky hands like magnets to the piles of flame-coloured leaves littering the ground. Now at home washed, lunched, and healthily tired, they slept well.

Before working on the new project planning I reflected on the day. It had challenged me, finding this new area, planning the route, and driving it with two lively children, and being up early to bake before the children woke. I smiled as I remembered the fun we had throwing the autumn leaves over us. I felt good, nature had enriched me, my early morning baking although a bit rustic-looking proved deliciously moreish. I felt an overwhelming sense of gratitude and contentment we had had so much enjoyment from such a simple activity.

The most important criteria for these projects, was that it should be something I had never done before. It could be craft of some sort, an educational endeavour, cooking, innovation, exploring, or simply a walk in a park—a park I had never been to. But each activity involved four key steps.

- ♥ Intention or conception
- ♥ Planning
- ♥ Event/activity
- ♥ Reflection or review

It could be a small task or a sizeable enterprise over a few days, but even with time-consuming projects, these four steps were paramount in the daily activity. At first, because of my physical limitations, the projects were simpler and less demanding in nature, but as my mobility returned I was able to do more challenging tasks.

Because each DCP was relatively short in duration, there was no time for it to become an anti-climax or routine. It was not a craft or enterprise fit for an exhibition or award—it was homespun. Each DCP was fun, while not always perfect, but always enjoyable. The enjoyment came from the focus I gave each effort. It gave me purpose. It filled my mind with a constructive focus, dispelling any thoughts of disability and grief.

Pivotal to the success of these DCP's was intention. My intention or concept always included visualizing the delight and fun of the activity, and seeing a positive end result.

I loved the planning too, the steps needed to put it all into motion. It appealed to my sense of order. I love a well-planned checklist that makes endeavours happen seamlessly.

After each project, I took time to feel the buzz of completion. Whether there were tangible results or simply a happy memory it didn't matter, as I felt satisfied and had a sense of coming home to myself

'How do you dream them up every day?' my friends asked. My immediate response was, 'creativity begets creativity,' but although it was a pretentious reply, I honestly did believe this and still do. There was always a steady stream of potential projects filling my mind. Not always big, not always too challenging—it might be simply trying out a new recipe and dishing it up with attitude, (I may well have been one of the first cooks to deconstruct a dish which is so fashionable in restaurants today), changing the furniture in the lounge, to give it fresh perspective or doing simple craftwork with the children. It simply did not matter—the exercise was in the intention, planning, enthusiasm and absorption in the activity and satisfaction from a job well done.

I found instead of my mind fixed on my loss and health, I was taking control and determining what gave me pleasure and contentment. Yes of course I was still overwhelmed with sadness and hopelessness from time to time, but my focus was on the higher good, and not stuck on the treadmill of poor me.

With every passing week I was feeling more alive, healthier, more in tune with my life. Steadily developing a sense of esteem, I was not only coping with being a single parent, but also relishing the responsibility.

Why do I think doing a daily creative project was so effective for me?

As a small child, I remember making things out of the odd bits of flotsam that came my way. My playmate was my imagination in the form of my imaginary friend. Creativity had always made me happy and somehow safe; throughout my young life I had written short stories, used a needle and thread for embroidery, or created patchworks from bits of recycled fabric, knitting, flower arranging, writing scripts for family play acting, and I was in seventh heaven with the feast of craft pre-Christmas. Each DCP gave me back a sense of childish wonder of being joyfully in the moment.

My mind was focused on my creativity, giving structure and order to the project, the delight in the activity, and finally basking in a job well done. Instead of the ancient part of my brain taking me down to the dark side, I was uplifted daily and if you do this often enough, you change your world.

Eckhart Tolle, wrote in his book *The Power of Now* and *A New Earth: Awakening to your Life's Purpose*: 'The past has no power over the present moment.' Yes—but I would add, especially when one's mind is focused on a daily creative practice.

Mihaly Csikszentmihalyi, (pronounced so delightfully Me-High-Chick-Sent-Me-High), is a Distinguished Professor of Psychology and Management at Claremont Graduate University in California USA. He is also the founder and co-director of the non-profit research institute Quality of Life Research Center that studies happiness and creativity.

Professor Csikszentmihalyi is particularly known for the development of his theory on 'flow.' 'Flow' is a psychological state in which individuals feel entirely and joyfully absorbed in an activity that challenges their skills and abilities. Athletes often refer to it as being in the 'zone.'

In his book *Flow; The Psychology of Optimal Experience*

published in 1990 Mihaly Csikszentmihalyi defined 'flow' as:

'The optimal state of experience is one in which there is order in consciousness. This happens when psychic energy—or attention—is invested in realistic goals, and when skills match the opportunities for action. The pursuit of the goal brings order in awareness because a person must concentrate attention on the task at hand and momentarily forget everything else. These periods of struggling to overcome challenges are what people find to be the most enjoyable times in their lives. By stretching skills, by reaching toward higher challenges, such a person becomes an increasingly extraordinary individual. 'Flow' is the way people describe their state of mind when consciousness is harmoniously ordered, and they want to pursue what they are doing for its own sake.'

In a nutshell, he describes, 'flow' as: 'Being completely involved in an activity for its own sake. The ego falls away. Time flies. Every action, movement, and thought follows inevitably from the previous one. Your whole being is involved, and you're using your skills to the utmost.'

The following is a quote from Csikszentmihaly's book *Creativity: Flow and the Psychology of Discovery and Invention*, published in 2008.

'Wake up in the morning with a specific goal to look forward to. Creative individuals don't have to be dragged out of bed; they are eager to start the day. This is not because they are cheerful, enthusiastic types. Nor do they necessarily have something exciting to do. But they believe there is something meaningful to accomplish each day, and they can't wait to get started on it. Most of us don't feel our actions are meaningful. Yet everyone can discover at least one thing every day is worth waking up for. It could be meeting a certain person, shopping for a special item, potting a plant, cleaning the office desk, writing a letter or trying on a new dress. It is easier if each night before falling asleep, you review the next day and choose a particular task that, compared to the rest of the day, should be relatively interesting and exciting. Then next morning, open your eyes and visualize the chosen event—play it out briefly in your mind, like an inner videotape, until you can hardly wait to get dressed and get going. It does not matter if at first the goals are trivial and not that interesting. The important thing is to take the easy first steps until you master the habit, and then slowly work up to more complex goals. Eventually most of the day should consist of tasks you look forward to, until you feel that getting up in the morning is a privilege, not a chore.'

Wow and double wow—as this old broad does a jig about the room, how amazing little old me knew what she was onto half a century back!

Double bonus for those of you who are in love with your yoga practice, it seems yoga is the perfect vehicle to get into the 'flow' for many people. The similarities between yoga and 'flow' are extremely strong. Csikszentmihaly said, 'It makes sense to think of yoga as a thoroughly planned 'flow' activity. Both try to achieve a joyous, self-forgetful involvement through concentration which is made possible by the discipline of the body.'

Michelangelo took five years of agonising work lying on his back on scaffolding, while lifting his arm to the heavens to create his masterpiece The Creation on the Sistine Chapel ceiling. He was so lost in his work he went without food, drink and sleep. When exhaustion took hold he fainted into sleep, and yet when he became conscious he was alert and refreshed and ready to paint once more. He had all the attributes of being in the 'flow.'

And it is not difficult to recognise musicians at one with their music—their eyes closed and faces shaped with bliss, seemingly only aware of the conductor's baton or emoting the lyrics. It is clear Charlie Parker, the legendary jazz saxophonist and composer, understood being in the 'flow' or 'groove' when he said, 'Music is your own experience, your thoughts, your wisdom. If you don't live it, it won't come out of your horn.'

But before you rush out to buy a yoga mat, easel or musical instrument—it is also doing simple things like playing a sport, sewing, cooking, singing, game playing, or making something that can get you into the 'flow.'

What excites me is Csikszentmihaly's directions to take you into this state of 'flow' compare well with the simple steps I was using fifty years ago.

- ♥ Decide on your activity. It can be anything from sporting activities to artistic endeavours you love doing.
- ♥ Get the challenge balance right. It should challenge you sufficiently to keep your attention. If it is too easy you will be bored, too difficult, and you will be overwhelmed. Aim for the baby bear option.
- ♥ Set goals. Be specific on what this activity aims to achieve, and how you know you are succeeding. If the activity is making a fancy cake, you know you are succeeding as you prepare the cake tin with baking paper, assemble and weigh your ingredients, cream the butter and sugar to a pale cream, fold in the flour in a figure of eight …

- ♥ Importantly, don't worry if it is not perfect—best not to have any pressure of expectations.

- ♥ Focus on the task at hand. Create the perfect environment so you can concentrate fully. Eliminate anything that will distract you—that includes the phone.

- ♥ Give yourself enough time. It takes about 15 minutes to get into the flow. But once you enter the flow state, you lose all sense of time as you become more and more fully immersed in your activity.

- ♥ Be aware of your emotional state. If you seem to be on track but not getting a sense of delight in super-concentration, then consider what may be going on for you—are you angry, worried, or simply low? Then take yourself for a walk in nature, or do something you know always lifts your spirits before trying again.

Put simply, being in the flow makes you happy!

Being happy is not just about feeling warm and fuzzy. Being happy improves health. Studies consistently show being happy lowers the risk of heart and other diseases, combats stress, strengthens the immune system, and lengthens our lives.

Yes, you've read this quote from Bruce Lipton in Chapter 3, but it is well worth repeating:

> 'Cells, tissues, and organs do not question information sent by the nervous system. Rather, they respond with equal fervor to accurate life-affirming perceptions and to self-destructive misperceptions. Consequently, the nature of our perceptions greatly influences the fate of our lives.'
>
> *Spontaneous Evolution: Our Positive Future*, Dr Bruce Lipton, published in 2006

Dr Herbert Benson, cardiologist, founder of Harvard's Mind/Body Medical Institute and author of *The Relaxation Response*, published in 1976, believes doing craftwork such as needlework, knitting, and crocheting can induce a relaxed state similar to meditation and yoga.

He says if you are learning, you need to push past the frustrating stage to get sufficient skill, and once there, these activities can lower heart rate, blood pressure, and reduce the levels of stress hormones.

Betsan Corkhill is a recognised world expert on the use of therapeutic crafts for improving health, wellness, and managing illness and is also the founder of 'Stitchlinks' a non-profit global support network. Corkhill and Cardiff University surveyed over 3,500 knitters and found 81% of the respondents said they felt happier and calmer during and after knitting. (Paper – published in British Journal of Occupational Therapy, February 2013.)

Like Benson, Corkhill has found knitting or crochet induces a meditative state of mind. She says, 'Knitting could enable a much wider population to experience the benefits of meditation, as it does not entail having to understand, accept or engage in a prolonged learning period of the practice. It happens as a natural side-effect of knitting.'

Interestingly, even Albert Einstein was reputed to have knitted between projects to calm his mind and clear his thinking.

Creativity is such a powerful tool—not only can it be used in healing for the sick, but it helps mend broken lives. I love this story of a musician who brought hope and a sense of renewal to a community.

On the 7th of February 2009, forever known as Black Saturday, an intense firestorm swept through the state of Victoria in Australia. The land, tinder dry, exploded in the path of the fires resulting in a loss of 173 lives and over 400 people injured. The fires destroyed several small townships, including the tiny tourist town of Maryville. You can only imagine the shock and grief of those who survived. Many—who had lost family, friends, neighbours, and their homes—escaped with only their clothes on their backs.

The survivors suffered what they called 'fire brain,' which included headaches, sleeplessness, tension, sadness, memory loss, and difficulty in concentrating. I am sure many would also have suffered from 'ambiguous loss.' Local musician Dr Rita Seethaler was determined to do something to help the bushfire affected families, and came up with an out-of-left-field Caribbean steel-pan band project.

The majority of people who joined the band had no musical background—they had to memorise songs and rhythm patterns, as well as learning new skills. It was hard at first, but eventually, they grew to make beautiful music.

'For a long time, we thought we'd never have joy in our lives again. But the sense of accomplishment the first time we conquered Bohemian Rhapsody was amazing. The band has rebuilt lives—made us happy again,' said one of the band members. Today, this one band has grown into three and gives concerts around Australia and overseas.

Fifty years ago, music and art therapy weren't even on the radar. Today, we are fortunate to access amazing art and music therapists who provide well-documented help to heal sick and broken lives. The skills, compassion, and dedication of these therapists and artistic endeavours bring hope and healing to many.

Over fifty years ago, my intuition, the unconscious me, said, 'Do something creative every day.' The only criteria it stipulated it should be something I had never done before. My daily creative projects distracted me from my poor health, they distracted me from my sense of loss, and from the anxieties of single parenthood.

Creativity—DCP's—gave me pleasure and purpose, and I thrived physically and emotionally. Like the steel pan band member, I too believe creativity gave me new hope to rebuild my life and made me happy again.

Chapter 9

The Elephant in the Room
Radically Changing Your Diet?

'Let food be thy medicine and medicine be thy food.'
Hippocrates

While I have ticked the boxes of most of the vital nine key factors that Kelly Turner's Radical Remission research has demonstrated, the numero-uno on this list is 'Radically changing your diet.' For many survivors of cancer or people managing chronic disease, diet is their first thought and action, and it is a proven life-changing step.

What we eat is now firmly linked to risks associated with ill-health in the Western world in the 21st century. It makes perfect sense that 'radically changing your diet' is a must in today's world. As well as dietary changes being a king hitter from the Heart Foundations, Diabetic Association, Cancer Council, Obesity Australia, and every other health authority. MS is no exception.

We are bamboozled by different types of diet – vegan, macrobiotic, raw food, Paleo, Mediterranean, high protein low carb, South Beach, Total Wellbeing, Weight Watchers, 5:2 Diet and the list of diets gets fatter with every scroll of the internet. Each of these diets, or eating plans, promotes that their specific diet is effective in improving our health. It is an overwhelming task for those, with limited dietary knowledge, to find the right eating solution to heal whatever is wrong with them. Thank goodness for nutritionists, naturopaths, herbalists, and other alternative practitioners.

Recently I had to change my way of eating—on my travels I picked up a nasty stomach bug called giardia, this wretched little critter was resistant to two courses of antibiotics. Finally, I was prescribed with what I can only describe as the nuclear bomb of an antibiotic, which meant swallowing four horse-size pills in one go. This annihilated the bug, but it also destroyed the natural flora and fauna of my gut. To renew the vital gut flora, I was advised by my doctor not to eat certain foods that would ferment in the gut. The results have been beyond my expectations of being stomach-cramp free—I felt more energized and alive, as well as the bonus of my body slowly shedding some excess kilos.

I have a new respect for my 6.5 metres of intestines. It seems that health specialists are saying gut health is the new medical frontier. I have more reading to do here I think.

A JOURNEY OF CREATIVE HEALING

Today, most of us are anxious about the quality of our food, and we view our supermarket produce warily. Our fears, real or unreal, hover around the possible use of chemical sprays, genetically modified foods, additives, and foods such as dairy, which has been manipulated to give us low-fat or no-fat products. To add to our sense of unease, our supermarkets scarily promote anti-biotic-free meat and chicken. We have learned to read between the lines of processed food packaging, as manufacturers hide the real breakdown of energy by foxing us with many different names for sugar—sucrose, fructose, dextrose, maltose etc. For those that can afford it, organic produce is their priority choice.

Fifty years ago, diet would not have been on the collective horizon, as a contributor to disease. Our diets in that time had been shaped by WWII. 'Dig for Victory' was a wartime catch-cry, and so the community tore up their flowerbeds and planted vegetables and fruit trees. The first six to eight years of my life we ate mainly vegetables and fruit, homegrown and tasty, and no pesticides. Wartime meat rationing was miserly, as was butter, and so my mother took our allowance in soup bones and made good quality stocks for casseroles with beans and vegetables. One egg a week per person did not go far, but this was supplemented with tinned powdered eggs. We ate a lot of fish, as this was not on ration. Bread was dense and salty (no talk of salt is bad for health back then), and even today I still miss the Hovis loaf, a small brown loaf of nuttiness and intensity, which my mother cut into lacy fine slices to eat with the vegetable casseroles.

I remember clearly the first and only times in my first eight years I ate a freshly boiled egg, the first time I had a piece of steak, the first time I ate a piece of chocolate, and an orange, which was a Christmas stocking treat. Rationing continued until I was sixteen, and so the nation continued to have a plain and reasonably healthy diet. It appears the British were at their healthiest in WW11. It goes without saying apart from the ubiquitous cup of tea, water was our drink of choice. In my family, we only drank alcohol on festive days, a sherry on Christmas morning or a whiskey with the Christmas cake or the occasional noggin on an evening out to the pub.

The English were used to home-grown produce, and by the 1960's most folk still grew these in their back gardens or on small parcels of land called allotments. The seasons controlled our eating—for the average family there was no expensive imported out of season fruit or veggies. Mind you, everyone had a chip saucepan! But for many postwar years, meat was not on the daily agenda for the average family—instead, egg and chips (one egg) or baked beans and chips became regular family meals. For my family, fish—as both parents were keen anglers—was the more frequent meal compared to our meat consumption.

Today, we eat whatever we like in large quantities. If you want cherries out of season in Australia, we can buy black fat juicy ones from California. Feel like asparagus out of season? Then buy cheap supermarket imports from Peru. You can get anything out of season, so much so the average young cook doesn't understand seasonality. Eating out is no longer nouvelle cuisine tiny portions of food set adrift on a large white plate. Our preference is more, the better. We all love to leisurely eat breakfast out at the weekend and the average cafe breakfast is a standard two golden eyed-eggs with multiple servings of bacon, sausages, hash browns, and a token tomato half gracing the white plate, which is now hardly visible for all the food. We eat too much and no longer eat sensibly.

Excess is the norm, and it is no wonder when ill-health strikes, we look to our diet.

I have hesitated to put too much emphasis on the disease called multiple sclerosis. Why? Because it was simply my 'vehicle' of illness, which had been given the diagnosis of MS. I still want to underline my belief that the symptoms of my ill health were a result of trauma and lifestyle. Whatever disease or illness that one is 'holding space,' it is obvious that the elements in recovery are similar to mine, but this key factor of 'radically changing diet'—the way I ate, so long ago—had no relevance.

But I think it only right, to introduce you to a medical specialist who has healed himself of MS—by primarily changing his diet.

Professor George Jelinek, in his early sixties, runs and swims regularly and says he has never felt healthier. In 1999, he was diagnosed with multiple sclerosis. This was a devastating blow for him, as he had watched his mother battle the disease for sixteen years, and when she could no longer take the pain or the dependence on others she took her own life. At the time of his diagnosis, he was the professor of Emergency Services at a leading hospital in Perth. He was 45 years old, and a family man with three children.

Immediately, he researched all he could on the disease and his findings led him to the work of American neurologist Roy Swank, who had published a paper in the Lancet 1990 'Effect of Low Saturated Fat Diet in Early and Late Cases of Multiple Sclerosis.' After many years of refining his findings on his seven-year recovery back to health, Professor George Jelinek wrote his first book *Overcoming Multiple Sclerosis*, published in 2016, which features his seven-step program for recovery. This program is widely accepted as an excellent way to manage the disease. It has been tried and tested by many sufferers around the world who have found considerable benefits from living this lifestyle.

These steps included:

- ♥ Changing your diet. Like Kelly Turners' findings, he does recommend the use of quality supplements like Omega-3 fatty acids and Vitamin D

- ♥ Exercise regularly. Thirty minutes a day, five days a week

- ♥ Sunbathe. Get enough sun fifteen minutes of sunlight, five times a week

- ♥ Meditating

- ♥ Change your life. Make sure you are number one in your life

All the medical evidence is showing conclusively that diet changes are effective on the road to healing serious illnesses. First, it means you are making decisions to take control of your illness, and second, a better quality and choice of food can only help with the healing process.

I would add this caveat to this chapter; I am dragging the chain a bit about food issues being constantly front and foremost in our collective consciousness. Making informed food choices, and improving our diet, can only be good. But to regularly view food as a potential hazard, and be 'on guard' every time you eat, cannot be good. Remember Bruce Lipton's words 'Cells, tissues, and organs do not question information sent by the nervous system...' There is a fine line between choosing to eat healthily and becoming obsessed with what we eat—we need to be mindful of the definition we give to food, and where we rest our minds.

I wonder if you remember the 2004 movie *Super-Size Me*? Morgan Spurlock is a documentary filmmaker, who creates a different beat of filmmaking, as he examines social issues in a way that make them engaging and entertaining to an audience. His film, *Super-Size Me*, became the highest grossing documentary of all time, and more importantly, changed the eating habits of millions.

Spurlock set himself the task of eating only McDonald's food for 30 days. The results of the fast-food diet showed that he gained 11.4 kilograms (25 pounds), his cholesterol levels rose dangerously high, and the doctors attending him, warned that his liver was 'turning to pâté.'

Following the release of this documentary, a Washington, DC-based group—Physicians Committee for Responsible Medicine (PCRM)—created a thirty-nine-second shock advertisement, titled *Consequences: I was lovin' it*. The film shows a hospital room—surrealistic music accompanies the visual of a man's dead body, lying on a stretcher—a half-eaten hamburger still in his hand. His grieving young wife stands beside the gurney. An edgy voice-over emphasises the text: 'HIGH CHOLESTEROL, HIGH BLOOD PRESSURE, HEART ATTACK—TONIGHT MAKE IT VEGETARIAN.'

While I value Spurlock's artistic efforts, to make us think about the perils of an extremely high-fat diet, I find the subsequent provocative add made by the PCRM, perfectly illustrates my thoughts that seeing food as the demon can frighten, and stress us unduly, doing us more harm than the occasional bite of fast food.

Moderation in all things, I say, is the best way.

Chapter 10

The Six Steps to Healing

'Experience is, for me, the highest authority. The touchstone of validity is my own experience. No other person's ideas, and none of my own ideas, are as authoritative as my experience. It is to experience that I must return again and again, to discover a closer approximation to truth as it is in the process of becoming in me.'
Carl Rogers—Founder of the Humanistic Psychology Movement

This book has been in a holding pattern in my mind for best part of a decade before I put pen to paper. It has proved to be an incredible journey of affirmation and discovery. As I began the substantial task of reading and researching, I was rewarded with a bounty of scientific and anecdotal evidence that confirmed my intuitive approach to healing fifty years ago.

But now, it seems equally relevant my trust and commitment to my questing nature that all would be well so many years ago did not need the scientific nod of confirmation.

Bottom line—I write it for others, in the hope they will find my journey of a creative healing helpful. And that it inspires others to trust their intuition and choose their own paths back to health.

Step 1. Acceptance: Accepting Responsibility

This was the first step I needed to take before my body and spirit could heal. It was the hardest step to achieve, as it was not just accepting responsibility for my state of health—it was accepting a frightening burden of sole responsibility for my children's upbringing.

I was in emotional lockdown. And conscious, as in knowing, I was not.

Taking responsibility—for me—did not mean simply that I decided on a course of healing action. It meant that I needed to emotionally come to a point of acceptance that I was spiritually, psychologically, as well as physically, central to the disease's cause—and then—to its subsequent outcome.

I understood intellectually the concept of taking responsibility for my life and its benefits of clarity and release that it would give me, but I needed to break through the layers of trauma for my heart to accept who I was, where I was, and how I was. Fortunately, I was resilient and always had a powerful conviction that I would reach a place of acceptance. And it came, after weeks of quiet bed rest, when I had given up the fight within myself.

Many people, will think ill-health is simply bad luck, or a

series of health issues, or genetic heritage, and they will be more comfortable taking the conventional medical path, finding the right physician and working with his/her best intentions to bring them back to health.

As you have read, Peter my current husband has had two major heart operations over the past twenty years and is committed to his cardiologist's instructions on medication. He and his present cardiologist believe his genetic history and poor stress management are the major factors in his heart problems. Happily, for Peter, he has a strong conviction that doctor knows best, and this works well for him—with every annual cardio check-up he gets a good result. And he would not stray from conventional medicine.

What is evident is the critical role chronic stress plays in the road to ill-health. Science tells us an overload of stress causes us to flood our systems with cortisol, which is not good for our health. Add to this our brains—well the oldest part of the brain called the limbic—determinedly revels in the bad stuff, and skims over the good stuff, which means we can easily get addicted to everyday stressors.

Science again told us how our cells and organs simply respond to the conscious and unconscious messages we send to them and responds in equal function to either positive or destructive thought.

But then the good news came in the form of putting a spin on how we deal with stress. If we see it as a challenge other than a threat, we recover more effectively from the 'fight-or-flight' response. Indeed, it was found reasonable bursts of 'challenge-stress,' with a recovery period in between, is similar in value to physical exercise, and can make us stronger.

An important stage for me was the extended quiet time of rest. The old proverb said it well 'silence is golden' and science is now proving what the formidable 19th-century nurse Florence Nightingale promoted—that quiet is an essential part of care for patients in recovery. During this period of quiet, scientists observe the brain is reflecting on 'self,' in a productive, non-egotistical manner.

Looking back through time, I can understand how this quiet resting time allowed me to process my wounds at an unconscious level to enable me to reach the benefaction of acceptance.

Step 2. A Spiritual Wake-up Call and Finding the Silver Lining

This chapter's proposition of a spiritual wake-up call, is thin on scientific fixing but it is of no consequence, I'm sure so many of us know people who, after trauma or severe illness, have dramatically done an about-turn in their lives. It is no surprise people faced with crisis do something different, from the way they have always done things. Commonsense tells you loudly and clearly, doing it the same old way, just ain't working for you.

People faced with life-threatening illnesses are at the tipping point of embracing change. For me, the changes were complex—it was learning to be an adult, accepting my loss, becoming aware of who I was, and who I was becoming.

Grief is the greatest leveler. But I am grateful this searing loss gave me back deep, pure, drifts of compassion, understanding, and love. It was the silver-lining of the horrendous calamitous event.

Aunty G was my beacon of hope. She was the only one who had a handle on how it was to have one's hopes and dreams slashed beyond measure. She told me the truth—not some flowery version all would be well—but straight from one widow to another, left with small children to raise. But in this potpourri of pick-yourself-up-and-get-on-with-your-life, she added, 'Find the silver-lining, there is always a silver-lining.'

The modern-day psychology is saying gratitude (silver-lining) can make you happy, and happiness, as we have seen in Chapter 8, helps you to heal.

Don't confuse positive thinking with the practice of gratitude. Being positive is our attempt to control our responses to life's challenges. It may work for a while, but the dinosaur brain is a determined little sucker who undoubtedly wants to dance in the mire of doom and gloom, and poof goes your all your good will and intentions.

Gratitude requires self-reflection. Frequently it requires digging deeper to find it. Often having to traverse anger, doubt, and pain leaves us to focus on what is good, what is beneficial, and what is it that makes you truly thankful. And the benefits of a regular 'silver-lining' practice are many. Science tells us it will improve our physical and psychological health, develop better relationships, and help us to become more resilient. For that, I am very grateful.

Step 3. Not buying into the diagnostic label

Many who view the medical world, as the absolute authority on health may be uncomfortable with this particular step—even seeing my rejection of the diagnosis of multiple sclerosis as foolhardy and irresponsible.

But nevertheless, it was right for me and from my research, it was right for others too, who turned their back on the conventional healing methods and found their own way back to health. I know if I had embraced the treatment, joined a support group and lived my life through this narrow prism of multiple sclerosis, my life would have played out very differently.

When my doctor delivered the verdict of my two neurological examinations, I received it, with what I can only describe, as stoic inflexibility. 'Come to the surgery and we will talk about treatment—and I will put you in touch with a support group who will help you become more at ease with the disease.' (Well, words to that effect—after all it was half a century ago) I said nothing, I was intransigent, and I knew I was not going to the treatment appointment nor that I would ever join a support group. My mind was silently and doggedly repeating 'NO.'

Denial?

While it may well have been denial, I think my previous 'nocebo' (Latin – 'I will be harmful') event of Bell's palsy instantly sliced and diced those experiences, and my instincts delivered the message on cue.

Placebo (Latin –'I shall please') goes hand-in-hand with the control studies on drugs and we have all heard incredible stories about the healing power of the placebo—whether it is in a drug trial, sham surgery, or a physician who shows you a depth of caring. From my reading, I gather that we are at the gateway to discovering the potential of placebos.

An aside here – research is proving, that when you take a drug or supplement if you set your intention to receive it as an agent of healing while in a quiet and reflective state—the medication is even more efficacious.

Now although the scientific world knows the nocebo can be equally effective, there are few trials and studies. It was a challenge to do the placebo studies because of the ethics involved—hoodwinking patients being central to these concerns. These issues are made even more difficult in nocebo studies as these trials could very well harm the volunteers. But nevertheless, the nocebo effect is recognised and understood by science.

This chapter also touches on the work of Professor John Ioannidis and his team, who diligently review published papers of studies and trials from around the world to determine whether the outcomes are without bias, exaggeration, or flaws. Ioannidis believes an overwhelming amount of these published papers—which doctors rely on—are flawed. While it is not difficult to understand, even with the best intentions, bias does occur, whether consciously or unconsciously, it is yet another setback to the credibility of medical data, which features so frequently in our media. But the important point to take from this is the medical world highly respects Ioannidis 's work, and they see the intrinsic value of his mission to determine and promulgate the accuracy of studies and trials.

My premise—and of others who have the additional qualification of being well versed in quantum physics and are of more authority than I—is that we are energy that attracts like energy. In other words, our focus creates our reality. A bit new age? Think again—Albert Einstein one the world's greatest minds, said 'Everything is energy and that's all there is to it. Match the frequency of the reality you want and you cannot help but get that reality. It can be no other way. This is not philosophy. This is physics.' In other words, 'What worries you, masters, you.' This quote was delivered in the 17th century by John Locke, a physician, and philosopher, and lauded to be the most influential thinker of his time.

Anecdotally, I have known many people in my lifetime who have embraced a diagnosis, and in a mature fashion have followed the bouncing ball of conventional treatment with good results. For many, this works, and my stance of not buying into the diagnosis would be intolerable.

So, this chapter is not a judgment on others who do not hear the same call. We are each different, and we must go home to health in our own ways. Like my friend Patty, who has suffered throughout her life from complex colon disorders. For her, an accurate diagnosis, allowed her to come to terms with her illness and gave her the scope to self-manage her chronic illness successfully.

For me—who is more than susceptible to both placebo and nocebo effect—choosing to debunk the diagnosis and say my sickness was about shock, lifestyle, and fear, was a major step in turning my back on a chronic disease.

Or, as another radical remission cancer survivor was intuitively told, not to call it cancer—instead he was 'holding the space for cancer.' Equally, I was simply holding the space for MS.

Step 4. Grief, Surrender, and Stillness

Those who have experienced losing a loved one will know that grief is not tidy, compartmentalized, or lasting a prescribed duration of time. It is the most chaotic mess of emotions, with no time constraints, that you will ever experience, and each of us tackles it in the only way we know how.

You read that the passage of grief can get even more compromised when you are stuck—frozen in time you might say. Dr Pauline Boss, was an undergraduate when she developed the theory of 'ambiguous loss.' Today, she is a leader in this work, helping the bereaved come to terms with events such as 9/11 terrorist attack on the World Trade Centre, as families attempt to comprehend the fact, that there is nothing left of their loved one to mourn.

Stumbling upon Dr Boss's work was a gift. This was a powerful finding for me—all of the pieces of my conflict with grief fell into place, giving me a 'light-bulb' moment of clarity – recognising the reason that I was stuck, for so many years, on an emotional treadmill of denial, guilt, anger, and depression. It also allowed me to understand why my children throughout their lives, have felt the loss so keenly when my rational mind said they did not know him.

It helped me comprehend, why my daily creative projects bought comfort to my grief—they gave my life meaning and new hope.

Stillness and Surrender

The first few years, after Robert's death, was filled with exhaustion—as I hung on grimly, caring for my children and in constant conflict with my grief. But with the knowledge, that I had done all I could to set my life straight, and having the support from my family, I was able to be drift deeper into the balm of quiet, in my bedroom retreat.

You read earlier that I took to my bed for many hours a day in the first months when the symptoms were severe. Each day, with the nurture of stillness and deep rest, I was growing a little stronger. The months of my hibernation and gradual recuperation meant I spent considerable time in meditation in the quiet of my bedroom. I did not identify this quiet concentration on my breathing, as meditation then, but looking back now it is obvious.

Meditation is when the brain is not dishing up the norm, but is deeply quiet or scientifically termed, in a 'theta' state. There are many varieties of meditation and mine was simple, I liked to concentrate on my breathing, simply focusing on the breath.

Science is still making up its mind how best to test the effectiveness of meditation, mindfulness, and other mind-body therapies such as yoga. Yet there is enough empirical evidence out there for the medical world to see value in these therapies.

A JOURNEY OF CREATIVE HEALING

Dr Herbert Benson, whom you met formally in Chapter 8 - The Benefits of Creativity, is the author of *New York Times* bestseller *The Relaxation Response* published in 1976. Basically the 'relaxation response' is an easy, convenient, and time-friendly meditation, which is quick to learn, and if practiced ten minutes a day, can treat the harmful effects of stress. This therapeutic practice is often routinely recommended to treat patients suffering from heart conditions, high blood pressure, chronic pain, insomnia, and many other physical ailments.

9 Steps to Elicit the Relaxation Response

1. Pick a focus word, short phrase, or prayer that is firmly rooted in your belief system.
2. Sit quietly in a comfortable position
3. Close your eyes
4. Relax your muscles, progressing from your feet to your calves, thighs, abdomen, shoulders, head, and nec
5. Breathe slowly and naturally, and as you do, say your focus word, sound, phrase, or prayer silently to yourself as you exhale
6. Assume a passive attitude. Don't worry about how well you're doing. When other thoughts come to mind, simply say to yourself, 'Oh well', and gently return to your repetition
7. Continue for 10 to 20 minutes
8. Do not stand immediately. Continue sitting quietly for a minute or so, allowing other thoughts to return. Then open your eyes and sit for another minute before rising

9. Practice the technique once or twice daily. Good times to do so are before breakfast and after dinner

From *The Relaxation Response*, Dr Herbert Benson, published 1976

Step 5. Trusting and Acting Upon Intuition

Intuition is no longer viewed with a jaundiced eye; science is now showing us intuitive thinking is often better than poring over reams of data to make the decision. For some time, the world's greatest brains—such as Einstein, Salk, Jobs, and Branson—have respected and called upon their intuition to give them answers.

MRI scans show intuition emanates from deep in the brain in an area called the insula. The insula is the centre of all ranges of emotions, including the pleasure of music and appreciation of wine. It is believed we draw on all of our past experiences to give us an instant prompt message. Evidently, our brain uses simple rules of thumb to seek an intuitive solution or answer. For instance, the fielder in the cricket team who makes a seemingly impossible catch does not employ mammoth calculations of height, distance and rate of fall—instead he follows two simple rules of thumb—keeping an eye on the ball and maintaining the angle while running in the direction of the ball.

Intuition can come loudly to us in a crisis, but often the soft voice of intuition is ignored as the sophisticated part of our brains tries to use logic to override it. Richard Branson trusts his intuition above the cleverest of accountant's advice when he is making business decisions, and Einstein—for all his amazing thinking capacity—trusted answers, that came out of the blue when he was working on finding a solution to a challenge

Meditation helps us access it, and practice will develop it.

In this chapter we have seen how listening and acting on our intuition makes dramatic life changes, and uses leaps of imagination to provide accurate information. I think that the biggest hurdle with intuition is having the courage to act upon it. But the more you trust it, the more it delivers.

Step 6. Focusing on Creativity

I hope you felt my enthusiasm come through my words as I attempted to tell you how much joy the daily creative projects gave me. I tackled projects, which ranged from simple to complex, or bigger challenges—and these gave me focus on a goal outside of myself, rather than on the reality of my circumstances.

Each daily activity comprised of four steps—intention or concept, planning, activity, and review. The projects did not have to be perfect—in all honesty, they were homespun in nature—but this did not matter. It was the consistency and fulfillment of the exercise that worked its healing magic.

So, does science share my belief, creativity is not only rewarding but also healing? While there are not the scientific trials specific—to creativity equals healing—there is evidence being in the 'flow' of creativity makes us happy. Also, creativity in the form of craft, work, art, music, cooking and other activities will elicit not only happiness but provides the added bonus of creating a meditative state.

We do not need a panel of white-coated scientific bods to

tell us that daily helpings of focus on what makes us happy, which takes us into the beneficial theta waves of meditation, is bound to improve our health and sense of well-being.

I love the fact, that 81% out of the study of 3,500 knitters said they felt happier and calmer during, and after knitting. I love the fact, that Einstein knitted between projects to calm his mind and clear his thinking.

To round off this valuable and rewarding support for creativity, was the story of the small township that was destroyed in a firestorm in the bushfires that raged through a small town in Victoria Australia, burning all in its path. Families lost everything, including family members, friends, and neighbours.

A local musician, seeing their grief and depression, set up a Caribbean steel pan band project. The challenge and making of beautiful music brought the town back to life. They felt a sense of achievement and joy especially when they mastered *Bohemian Rhapsody*.

My DCPs were one of the tools in the mix of healing methods—taking responsibility, rest and reflection, rejecting the diagnostic label, finding-the-silver-lining, meditation, and intuition—but this step was the icing on the cake, the one that took me over the line into health.

The final step was where I could chart my progress from projects that took into account my bung arm and gammy leg through to knitting squares, walking without a limp and speaking without slurring my words. And most importantly, I was now relishing my role as a single parent. Not much for most healthy folk, but to me, it was as if I had climbed the tallest mountain and stuck the flag in the peak.

Chapter 11

Living and Learning

'The act of going within, finding our truth, and then sharing it, it helps us far more than we know.'
Kamal Ravikant, Live Your Truth

Without the searing intervention of the loss of Robert, I might never have had the courage, drive, or understanding to leave the comfort of my cocoon to begin the journey of spiritual evolution.

As Socrates, the father of western philosophy said, 'The unexamined life is not worth living.'

The harshness of grief and illness marked a line in the sand. It spun me around and I could no longer tread the boards of my life beforehand. I was a different person. I now had glimpses of the authentic me, a softer, kinder person, and wanted more.

This was the beginning of a lifetime journey to seek my authentic Self.

Five years after Robert's death, I married Peter, my second husband. I had taken the children for a holiday with friends who lived in Nassau in the Bahamas. The month-long holiday turned into a year, after I met Peter, an English accountant, and fell in love.

The weather was wretchedly hot that July day in 1968 at Nassau Cathedral, in the Bahamas, when we married. The sweat ran off us in rivulets. On the steps of the cathedral, guests covered us with confetti, and Peter's sodden white dinner jacket turned into a pastel artwork.

Our two-week honeymoon in Mexico was more a fiasco than a fiesta. The air, so thin in Mexico City—with its altitude of 2,250 metres above sea level—gave us mega-thumping headaches and nausea as we walked the ancient Aztec city. By the end of the first week, our energy was kaput. We decided that Acapulco, on the coast of Mexico, would be a kinder option. Day one was magic, walking the beach hand-in-hand, watching the fearless team of divers from the cliffs of La Quebrada, and eating from the roadside stalls ... Yes, you guessed it our altitude discomfort was nothing compared to suffering food poisoning aptly titled 'Montezuma's Revenge.' The rest of holiday was spent sprinting to the bathroom.

Our honeymoon set the tone for those early days, as we tried so hard to become a pop/mom family. To have another authority in the home was foreign to Jo, Neil and me, who knew of no other way for our threesome than 'all for one and one for all.' When Tania was born a year later, it helped us bond as a family, but the pressures and dynamics of a blended family are never easy, especially when children are deprived of knowing their biological father and when the ghost of his image was a constant in family life—until Peter.

It showed me clearly the grief of losing a parent at a young age continued to play out throughout their lives. Always the question lurking in the shadows for these children was 'would my life be different if 'he' were here?' Jo and Neil now are in their fifties, and despite all the slings and arrows of outrageous fortune, they have grown into decent, caring and functional adults. All three of my children are gifted with supportive and loving partners and broods of gorgeous children.

Following our years in the Bahamas we immigrated to Australia, bought a house, settled Jo and Neil into new schools, and after Tania began school I found a part-time job to supplement Peter's earnings. We developed a social life. Life was full and left little time for contemplation of my navel

But a navel-gazer I have been and always will be and at a deep level, I was still engaged on a journey to know my true self.

In Australia, I found God again—well religion.

I joined our local Protestant church—a 'high' church in the tradition of the ceremony, vestments, incense swinging, and a choir with voices, which uplifted the most miserable of spirits. For seven years, first I, and then Peter embraced church life, becoming regular worshippers and involved in every aspect of church life. I was a member of the Parish Council, I was on flower list, the baking list, and whatever other list that was going—as well as organising the annual Street Fair.

I loved the ritual of the service, the music, and the solemnity of worship, but hated the sermons that I always took personally. I never could call myself a Christian in the sense of the expected do-gooder, so I spent seven years working on my feelings of guilt and trying to change into what I believed a stereotypical Christian should be. I was, any shape but circular—peg in a round hole. Also during this time my conflict with the hypocrisy of a male-dominated religious institution, was growing steadily.

My holy high days drew to a close.

But the experience of religious self-reflection was not wasted. The layers began to lift. I saw how much my ego/identity sabotaged my efforts to belong—the aching longing to be recognised and the ever treadmill of not being enough. Becoming more conscious of this limiting belief pattern served me well. I was stronger and more resilient to life's speed bumps.

I was Peter's first love, and his loyalty and support have always given me the foundation of emotional security I craved. He was there for me when I went into dark days during two years of group therapy. In this group work, I became conscious of the individuals who triggered and fueled my feelings of not belonging and being unrecognised. A couple of days after group work were always hard, but somehow or other I always pulled through. It taught me one my best lessons in life, to trust that dark space, as confusion always comes before clarity or a breakthrough.

I was growing.

Strangely, in this mix of one-step forward, two back, I developed a serious fear of flying. If we had to fly I became almost catatonic for days before the flight. On the flight itself, I was sprung like a cat ready to pounce, convinced if I could maintain this vigil for the entire flight we would be safe. My lovely local doctor trained me in self-hypnosis. Then flying was no longer a white-knuckle ride for me and again it reminded me to trust all would be well.

A weekly-guided meditation group took me to another level of gentle growth. Gradually, parts of my pattern were simply lifting, as though they had never been.

Life was flowing, children were growing, and I was working and rising on the corporate ladder to a national position.

But within two years, I quit my prestigious job. I saw my life as useless. 'Who am I, what am I?' whirled in my mind. The answer always—I am nothing. I saw it as my mid-life crisis. For two years I did temporary jobs. I cried on buses as I travelled to and from jobs. Then we went on holiday to Europe, and the depression and uncertainty cleared.

It was our first trip back to our homeland twelve years after we arrived in Australia. The northern hemisphere holiday with the soft long twilight days of summer, the history and the culture of Europe gave me new impetus.

I knew I wanted to go back and do some further education. I chose Home Economics—I thought it was the best option as I was a good cook. Little did I know what an exacting discipline I had chosen.

Apart from my studies to become a home economist, I still wanted to work on tearing down the façade of Mary—the dysfunctional pleaser who so desperately wanted to be liked and recognised.

I read all the new age psychological and spiritual books I could find. One that particularly engaged me, was the autobiography of German Psychiatrist, Fritz S Perls—*In and Out of the Garbage Pail*, published in 1969.

Fritz—I could no longer address him formally as Dr Perls, after reading his all-embracing book, as I thought of him as a trusted friend—was the founder of Gestalt Therapy. The focus of Gestalt therapy is becoming aware of your feelings, emotions, and perceptions. In a nutshell, once you get past all of the existential psycho-jargon it is simple it is creating a dialogue with whatever is troubling you.

Put out the do not disturb sign and sit with an empty chair facing you. Imagine—whatever problem is troubling you—is a person sitting in the opposite empty chair. Now you role-play, out loud. At first, it seems ridiculous asking questions to and fro, but stick with it—you will find it will open your mind to the underlying issues effectively. I still use this technique when I need it.

I completed a six-week course on Sacred Geometry called the Flower of Life. 'All you need is a protractor and sketchpad,' the literature said. My geometry vocabulary was limited to acute angles and parallel lines, but I hung in there, learning about the star tetrahedron and within its mystical shape I believed I reached the nirvana of spinning my Merkabah. Although intellectually I found it challenging, it was gentle process, unlike the confronting group therapy.

(The Merkaba is an energy field that is comprised of specific sacred geometries that align the mind, body, and heart together. When it is activated as in 'spinning' it transports one to higher thoughts, lessons, and states of being.)

After I qualified, in the mid 80's, I founded my own business, first as an agency for home economists. In the late 80's and early 90's, Australia suffered the worst recession since the Great Depression in the early 1930s. Nobody was employing,

A JOURNEY OF CREATIVE HEALING

and if they did home economists were a luxury no company could afford. By then, I had smart offices and test kitchens, but zero work coming in.

Instead, we created our own work, in the form of Consumer Advisory Kitchens—small mobile kitchens located in shopping centres throughout Australia. Back in the test kitchens, we designed recipes around the shopping centre's food retailer needs, with recipes reflecting their primary markets purchases. This meant all during this time of scant employment, we kept 70 food professionals employed in regular casual work and 4 fulltime home economists as the backbone of the project. Over its thirty-year span, the business faced many challenges but it grew and gained a solid respectable reputation. With each new twist and turn it tested me and I grew stronger. But I should add here, that while I was more confident, I was a typical woman of my generation, I still was a poor second at the business negotiation table.

For twenty years, I was a member of a speaking club. The lectern, for many years, terrified me, and I could hardly speak without shaking. Gradually, I learned to manage the stage fright and went on to become an Accredited Communicator, while winning several public speaking awards. I trained others to present, and I built a second career as an emcee and speaker. A natural flow-on was my first book *Finding Your Voice: Ten Steps to Successful Public Speaking*.

I still yearned to be more in tune with my spirit. A decade ago, I was introduced to a year-long spiritual self-development course, which had at its core, creating what you love by developing your intuition and focus—it seemed a perfect match. The year-long course, a misnomer but that was its title, was, in fact, a monthly three-day weekend, over a twelve-month period.

It proved to be a boot camp for the soul. Most of the other participants were young—often it seemed to me they spoke another language, and boy did a lot of my fears come up.

And it was here I learned to confront the daddy-of-all-fears in an exercise called 'The Arrow Break.'

An arrowhead was placed in the soft, supple part of my throat while the other end was lodged hard against a team partner's flat of their hand. I had to step out in faith—please God don't let it kill me—moving forward towards my partner, arrowhead at my throat, the shaft and feathers steady against his palm until the 27-inch wooden hunting arrow snapped in half. Crazy I know, but the unfolding of previous self-development incarnations stood me in good stead. I snapped that pesky arrow in half in my first attempt!

But the course wasn't all about giving me bragging rights—I learned to hold firm my focus on what I love, mastered new techniques to develop my intuition, and all of the above, made me stronger.

So, am I free of all negative stories? Free of self-sabotaging patterns? Have you heard that expression 'you can take the girl out of the country, but you can't take the country out of the girl'? Well just replace 'country' with 'hot-spot' and you have it. Which means from time to time, given half the chance, these hot-spot triggers would delight in sending me into the quicksand of self-doubt.

I am a work in progress, but I am more resilient these days and am able to make the choice not to allow other's perceptions or words define me. I am not afraid to speak up—to say no, not now, not anymore. I belong to me.

My biographical novel *Losing You*, was my first venture

into fiction a couple of years ago, and already in the back of my mind is the next novel storyline taking shape. But this book was insistent to be told first.

Today I focus on what my heart loves: sharing my life with Peter and when we are able, being with my family whom, apart from Tania and her family, are scattered across this vast continent. Since I was a small child I was always a scribbler and a storyteller, but now in retirement, I am able to indulge my insistent muse. Any scrap of natural talent I may have is supplemented with the joy of learning the craft of writing.

Add to this heady mix of creative expression are my speaking gigs on cruise liners. My area of expertise is the history, peoples, and culture of the South Pacific. I am in the 'flow' not only on stage but at home, reading and researching and creating eye-popping visual slides to enrich my 45-minute presentations to happy holiday passengers.

I believe everything that comes into our lives has a purpose—the trick, as Aunty G' said, is finding the silver lining.

The next stop at this pointy end of life is embracing the silver lining.

When my soul says its time.

Acknowledgements

I would like to thank all the people who encouraged and supported me throughout the writing and subsequent publication of this book. A huge vote of thanks must go to Kaz Williams, Creative Director of the Big Shed Creative Communications. She was Marketing Director with an international publishing house for 22 years before leaving to set up her boutique marketing and communication business. Besides holding my hand as I explored my publishing options she designed the cover and interior of the book and is the key player in bringing this book to print.

    I met Kimba Arem, (who wrote the beautiful Foreword to the book) in Kauai, one the islands of Hawaii some years ago. At that time, I was given as a birthday present a one-hour music therapy session with this incredibly talented and spiritual young woman. I came away from the session totally blissed and upon writing this book I asked her if she would be one of my pre-publishing readers. To my eternal gratitude, she not only read it but also graciously edited the manuscript and wrote the Foreword for me.

My gratitude knows no bounds for the experts and other radical survivors of life threatening diseases who have given me their approval to feature their work and stories in this book. Kelly Turner of the Radical Remission Project, Bruce Lipton–biologist, Dr Rick Hansen, Dr George Jelinek, Dr Robert Emmons, Dr Bernard Lown, Gerd Gigerenzer–Director at the Max Planck Institute for Human Development, Mihaly Csikszentmihalyi–psychologist, Dr Herbert Benson, Betsan Corkhill–world expert on therapeutic craft, John Pattison–Macmillan Cancer nurse specialist, Barbara Weibel of Hole in the Donut Cultural Travel, Neill Duncan–musician, Robert Rabbin–author and speaker, and my dear cruising friend, Patty.

To all the people who have read and given me such valuable feedback on the early drafts of the book–Kitty Fitzgerald-Kingma, Helen Campbell, Sue Waters, Lillian Gibson, Patty O', Tania Nash, Jackie Egger, and fellow authors Caroline Cummings, Peter Howard, Julie Hyndman and Maggie Christian–my heartfelt thanks. Without your objective eyes I would never have seen what was needed to be seen.

Lastly to my family, especially Peter, who by now, I am sure could easily recite word for word the narrative as he has listened to me reading and rereading it to amend or extend the prose. I must make special mention of my youngest daughter, Tania, and her family who have been my staunchest fans, yelling from the side-lines to tell it all. And last but always first, my thanks and eternal love to Jo and Neil and their families who are such a vital part of this story.

Bibliography

Antonovsky, Aaron
Unravelling the Mystery of Health: How People Manage Stress and Stay Well (San Francisco, Jossey-Bass Publishers, 1987)

Benson, Herbert
The Relaxation Response (Harper Torch, 1976)

Csikszentmihalyi, Mihaly
Flow: The Psychology of Optimal Experience (Harper Perennial Modern Classics, 2008)

Csikszentmihalyi, Mihaly
Creativity: Flow and the Psychology of Discovery and Invention (Harper Perennial, 2003)

Emmons, Robert
Thanks! How the New Science of Gratitude Can Make You Happier (Houghton Mifflin Company, 2007)

Gigerenzer, Gerd. *Gut Feelings: The Intelligence of the Unconscious* (Penguin Books, 2008)

Hansen, Rick
Hardwiring Happiness: The New Brain Science of Contentment, Calm and Confidence (Harmony 2013)

Iyer, Pico
The Art of Stillness: Adventures of Going Nowhere (Simon & Schuster, 2014)

Jelinek, George
Recovering from Multiple Sclerosis (Allen & Unwin, 2016)

Lipton, Bruce
The Biology of Belief: Unleashing the Power of Consciousness, Matter, & Miracles (Hay House, 2008)

Lipton, Bruce and Bhaerman, Steve
Spontaneous Evolution: Our Positive Future And the Way to Get There from Here (Hay House, 2010)

Lown, Bernard
The Lost Art of Healing: Practicing Compassion in Medicine (Ballantine Books, 1999)

Maclean, Paul D
The Triune Brain in Evolution: Role in Paleocerebral Functions (Springer, 1990)

Marchant, Jo
Cure: A Journey into the Science of Mind Over Body (Crown, 2016)

Perls, Fritz S
In and Out of the Garbage Pail (Gestalt Journal Press, Revised Edition 1969)

Pert, Candace B
Molecules of Emotion (Touchstone, 1999)

Rankin, Lissa
Mind Over Medicine (Hay House, 1969)

Turner, Kelly
Radical Remission: Surviving Cancer Against All Odds (HarperCollins, 2014)

Also by Mary Atkins

Losing You

Two weeks after the birth of her second child, Kate Sinclair's life is shattered when her young husband is killed in a plane crash in London. Her grief is compounded by the guilt of rejecting his sexual advances the night before he died and desperate to feel loved again, she embarks on a disastrous liaison that leaves her family and friends uneasy with worry.

Kate is unwilling to face her grief and its consequences until her deteriorating health and the growing concern of her friends force her to see a doctor leading to a diagnosis of multiple sclerosis. Determined that it is simply her body's way of shutting down from the pain of losing her husband and the responsibility of becoming a sole parent, Kate's attempt to refocus and deal with the disease on her own terms while raising two young children leads to unexpected results and perhaps another chance at love and life.

Set in England and Australia during the swinging sixties, it is an insight into how urban society's attitudes towards sex outside of marriage, unmarried mothers and illegitimacy shaped the lives of women at the time.

Losing You is a rich and complex novel. Deeply moving, it is a story of the courage of the human spirit in overcoming adversity and the redemptive power of love.

Also by Mary Atkins

Finding Your Voice:
Ten Steps to Successful Public Speaking

Have you ever been asked to address an audience? Did the prospect create butterflies in your stomach?

Don't worry - you're not alone! But help is on its way. *Finding Your Voice: Ten Steps to Successful Public Speaking* is the definitive self-help guide to presenting and public speaking. Finding Your Voice provides a comprehensive step-by-step approach to becoming an effective speaker, covering a range of public speaking challenges. Learn the importance of sound planning, how to project your voice, manage stage fright, make the most of audio equipment and more. It also includes inspirational advice from some of Australia's leading celebrity speakers.

Organised in two sections, Part One cover the ten confidence-building steps to becoming a successful speaker. Part Two provides practical tips for the ten most common speaking assignments from proposing a toast, the responsibilities of an emcee and presenting a eulogy through to workshop presentations, debates, formal speeches, media presentations and chairing meetings.

No matter what the occasion, *Finding Your Voice: Ten Steps to Successful Public Speaking* will help turn your good ideas into great speeches!

www.ingramcontent.com/pod-product-compliance
Lightning Source LLC
Chambersburg PA
CBHW031420290426
44110CB00011B/464